MUAY THAI
A Living Legacy

Kat Prayukvong &
Lesley D. Junlakan

ISBN: 978-974-9293-70-6

Spry Books

Published by Spry Publishing Co., Ltd.
440/7 Soi Ratchawithi 3, Ratchawithi Rd.,
Ratchatewee, Bangkok 10400, Thailand
Tel: (+66) 02-248-6888 Fax: (+66) 02- 247-4719
www.sprypublishing.com

First edition, 2001
Reprinted, 2002
Second edition, 2005
Reprinted, 2006
Reprinted, 2007

Color Separation and Printing in Thailand,
by Asia Pacific Offset Co., Ltd. www.asia-offset.com

The publisher welcomes inquires from individuals or organizations, retailers or wholesalers, regarding single- or bulk-purchase of this volume. (Discounted rates quoted on request.) Companies interested in acquiring the distribution and/or publishing rights in their own country should also contact the publishers.

Acknowledgements

We would like to extend special thanks to all of the following:
Peera & Siriporn Prayukvong for their inspiration and unfailing support
Kalayanee Kanchanadul for production advice
Nidda Hongwiwat for domestic and international administration advice
David Martin for international marketing advice

Research & Advice:
David Rogers, Mike Figurelli & Terry Tippies from TBA-USA
Dr.Kevin G.Celuch & Dr.Craig Cutbirth, from Illinois State Universiry
Ajarn Panya Kraitus

Additional Photos:
Jeerapun Kuntisilchai for coordinating photography & research
Sunti Sreekumkul for Past Greats Collection
Somkid Sattapan for cover, Removing of the Head Circlet & other photos
Sunthorn Keereerat & Bhinnasak Kaewyai from Saengdaed Studio for
additional Muay Thai Weapon photographs
Wiwat Udomgalayarak for providing historical pictures of Thailand
Konwipa Konsin, National Archives of Thailand; & Dhira Kaewprachan &
Surachai Oupachit from Division of Literature and History of Thailand; for
providing *Praya* Pichai Dab Hak photo
Lt. Col. Boonserm & Sgt. Boonluer Nontijan for arranging the models at
Bonanza Camp, Khao Yai
Praiwong Decha-narong for permission to use the grounds of the Bonanza
Hotel for outdoor photography

Background & Historical Advice:
M.N. Songsri Nopvong & Wanlapit Sodprasert
Head of Cultural Assets Department Dr. Wichid Sheeshoen, Wirat Kangkan &
Manoon Thongkamsuk, for their information on Muay Thai traditions
Ajarn Thanong Poompanich for historical advice and assistance with photos
taken in Lumpini Stadium
Col. Amnat Pooksrisuk, especially relating to *Muay* Korat

Thanks to:
Pareena Prayukvong for introducing Kat to Lesley
Tanden Poottan & Grant Supaphongs for introducing *Ajarn* Chaichalerm and
Ajarn Phitsanu to Kat
Paralada Prayukvong & Nittaya Wisetpong for back up support

Premkamon Tinakorn-na-Ayutthaya, Tul Hongwiwat, Dr.Suchai
Sriprachyaanunt, Kittiphan Suriyasak, Seeladaet Suwannakorn, Soontorn
Chantanetra, Sirimongkon Luksiripat, Samart Payak-arun, Kaosai Galaxy,
Somrak Kamsing, Chanita Prawpraykul, Mongkol Changnoi, Olivia Mak &
Niruebol Kongrut for their kind coperation

Contents

FORWARD - Ajarn Chai   8

INTRODUCTION   10

CHAPTER 1:
The History & Development of Muay   12

The Legend of Shaolin Temple   14
The Origins of *Muay*   16
History at a Glance   18
Early *Muay* Contests   22
Bound Fist *Muay*   24
Early Training Methods   26
Royal *Muay*   28
The *Muay* Renaissance: Rama V & Rama VI   30
Regional Varieties of *Muay*   32
Muay Chaiya   34
The First Permanent Arena   38
From Thailand to the World: Rama VII - The Present   40
Ancient *Muay*   46
Towards the Future   48
Gallery of Legendary *Muay* Heroes   50
Muay Arenas & Stadiums   54

CHAPTER 2:
Muay Outfit, Amulets & Incantations
61

Traditional *Muay* Outfit 62
Outfit of Professional Muay Thai Fighters Today 64
Outfit of Amateur Muay Thai Fighters Today 66
Amulets 68
Incantations 71

CHAPTER 3:
The Tradition of Wai Khru
72

The Concept of *Wai Khru* 74
Why *Wai?* 76
Informing the Spirits Ceremony 78
Initiation as a Trainee Fighter 80
Annual Homage-Paying Ceremony 82
Initiation as a Teacher 84

CHAPTER 4:
Pre-Contest Rituals
88

The Muay Thai Ring 90
Women and the Muay Thai Ring 92
Musical Accompaniment to Muay Thai 94
Approaching the Ring Rituals 96
Ritual Dance of Homage 100
Removal of the Head Circlet 106

CHAPTER 5:
Basic Muay Thai Skills
108

Warm-Up Exercises 110
Clenching the Fist 114
Hand-Wraps 115
Muay Thai Stance 118
Vulnerable Targets 120
Basic First Aid 122

Contents

CHAPTER 6:

Footwork   **124**

Muay Shuffle   127
Alternating Stance Footwork   132
Step-Slide Shuffle   133
Diagonal Footwork   134
Leg-Block Footwork   136
Boxing Skip   138
Leaping   139

CHAPTER 7:

Muay Thai Weapons   **140**

Punch   144
Straight Punch   146
Hook   148
Swing   150
Spinning Back Fist   152
Uppercut   154
Jump Punch   156
Overhead Punch   158

Elbow Strike   160
Elbow Slash   162
Horizontal Elbow   164
Uppercut Elbow   166
Forward Elbow Thrust   168
Reverse Horizontal Elbow   170
Spinning Elbow   172
Elbow Chop   174
Double Elbow Chop   176
Mid-Air Elbow Strike   178

Knee Kick   180
Straight Knee-Kick   184
Diagonal Knee-Kick   186
Curving Knee-Kick   188
Horizontal Knee-Kick   192
Knee Slap   196
Knee Bomb   200

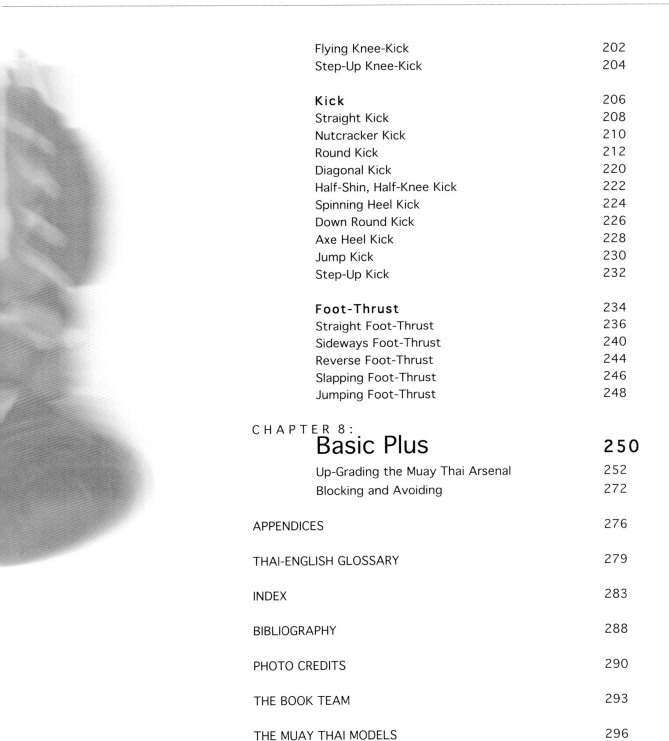

Flying Knee-Kick   202
Step-Up Knee-Kick   204

Kick   **206**
Straight Kick   208
Nutcracker Kick   210
Round Kick   212
Diagonal Kick   220
Half-Shin, Half-Knee Kick   222
Spinning Heel Kick   224
Down Round Kick   226
Axe Heel Kick   228
Jump Kick   230
Step-Up Kick   232

Foot-Thrust   **234**
Straight Foot-Thrust   236
Sideways Foot-Thrust   240
Reverse Foot-Thrust   244
Slapping Foot-Thrust   246
Jumping Foot-Thrust   248

CHAPTER 8:
Basic Plus   **250**
Up-Grading the Muay Thai Arsenal   252
Blocking and Avoiding   272

APPENDICES   276

THAI-ENGLISH GLOSSARY   279

INDEX   283

BIBLIOGRAPHY   288

PHOTO CREDITS   290

THE BOOK TEAM   293

THE MUAY THAI MODELS   296

THAI BOXING ASSOCIATION OF THE U.S.A.

P.O. Box 4585, Carson, CA 90749, USA   Ofc: 310/834-2724   Fax: 310/834-1580

Since going to live in the States over thirty years ago, I have had a mission -- if I can call it that -- to promote not only Muay Thai but also the country of my birth. Throughout those three decades, I have seen Muay Thai develop in the international arena from an almost unknown martial art to the well-established phenomenon which it is today, and I am happy to have been able to have played some small part in that growth.

I am often asked, "What are the benefits, what are the essential points of Thai boxing?" All the martial arts -- not just Muay Thai -- are not only about learning how to fight: they are also about self-discipline and self-awareness. My late father used to say that a Thai boxer should be "as soft as silk but as tough as a diamond." In other words, he should be outwardly humble and gracious but maintain an unshakable inner resolve and strict discipline: the two contrasting elements are, in fact, inseparable. So practicing Thai boxing skills is not just about physical exercise: it is also about mental training and getting to know who you really are as a person.

The training methods for Muay Thai differ from camp to camp, from gym to gym, and people often comment that this particular camp is especially strong on kicking techniques, that camp for punching and so on. There may well be some truth in this, but I also believe that your proficiency in using any particular Muay Thai weapon depends on yourself as much as anything else. To those of you who want to become really strong in Muay Thai, I would really like to recommend that you try to emulate the great boxers of a slightly earlier age. For *dhe* (kicking) look at Apidaet Sit-hilan; try to use *kow* (knees) like Diesel Noi; take Daenchai Yondaragit as your model for *sork* (elbows); and Samart Payak-arun, who also was great at movement and famed for his keen observation of his opponent, is the best possible teacher of *shok* (punching). Finally, for the general way of holding your body, of dodging and avoiding your opponent, take Adun Srisotorn and Sirimongkon Luksiripat as your role models. Learning from these great, great past masters is, I'm convinced, the best way to polish your own skills.

Nowadays, all kinds of people for all kinds of reasons are turning to Muay Thai. Just to give a few examples from my own experience: sportsmen from other fields practice Thai boxing to polish their skills -- the Dallas Cowboys, for instance, use it for conditioning, especially for footwork; more and more women are coming to the gym to learn Muay Thai for self-defense, when, in the event of an actual attack, its elbow and knee techniques would be particularly useful; officers from the armed forces and government agencies do Muay Thai training to improve their physique and reflexes; even movie stunt men realize the benefits of Muay Thai to increase their overall toughness! So, as you can see, it really is a martial art for everyone.

I have always been more than willing to help anyone involved in Thai boxing and its promotion in any way I can. I was particularly glad, therefore, when I was asked to assess and comment on this book before it went to press. For me, any book that helps to spread Thai boxing is a good book, but this one, I have to say, is really pretty special. It is strong both on photos and text: lots of pictures make it easy to understand and the explanations not only about the different techniques but also the cultural background are detailed and clearly presented. It is instructional and contains all anyone could wish to know about the basics of Thai boxing. In other words, it is a pretty good book for anyone interested in Muay Thai.

Enjoy reading *and* practicing...and good luck!

Surachai Sirisute, "Ajarn Chai"
President
Thai Boxing Association of U.S.A.
3rd May 2001
California, U.S.A.

Introduction

I t is now just over three years since the first edition of *Muay Thai: A Living Legacy* was published and, without any fanfare, started to appear on bookshop shelves. It was an up-hill struggle at first, trying to find markets for the book both here in Thailand and overseas. However, slowly but surely, people started to buy and spread the news that here, finally, was the in-depth book on the subject that everyone had been waiting for. It was given very positive reviews by Martial Arts magazines, trainers and practitioners of Muay Thai, especially in the USA, and became a best-seller on the subject at Amazon.com. We would like to thank the press, reviewers and, especially, martial arts fans for all their support and feedback. Judging from many comments, it seems that we did such a good job on researching and writing the book that some readers could not believe that it had been produced by two women outside Muay Thai circles.

The success of the book was a justification of all the time, experience and wisdom that so many people had given us since we met for the first time in May 2000 and agreed to start working on the project. Many of those same people must have quietly wondered how the pair of us could possibly succeed in the compilation and writing of such a book. Certainly it must have seemed a little strange: two women and one not even a Thai, entering the predominantly man's world of Muay Thai with very little previous knowledge or experience in the field. However, being relative outsiders had its advantages, as we were able to tackle the subject without preconceptions and probe in-depth, trying to answer all those *When...? Where...? Why...? What...?* and *How...?* questions which we had heard asked so often ourselves: "Why are women not allowed to enter most Muay Thai rings?" "What are the origins of Muay?" "Why do Muay Thai fighters perform the *Wai Khru Ram Muay* before each bout?" and so on.

In the three years since the first edition appeared, other Muay Thai books have been written and published and, believing that imitation is the sincerest form of flattery, we like to think that *Muay Thai: A Living Legacy* has helped pave the way for a resurgence of interest in not only the techniques of Muay Thai, but also in its history and traditions. Those years have also seen Lesley consolidate her position in the Martial Arts world, working as the cultural consultant for 3 documentaries (Muay Thai, Karate and Aikido) in *The Deadly Arts* series produced by a Canadian team and screened by National Geographic, and providing the English subtitles for *Khru* Lek's *Original Muay Thai* VCD. Kat has likewise been busy, obtaining her Masters in Media Studies at New School University in New York - - along with avidly promoting the book and networking among Muay Thai circles in the USA - - before finally returning to her base in Bangkok.

We now feel the time is right to set to work together on the long-awaited Volume 2 of *Muay Thai: A Living Legacy*, dealing, among other things, with Advanced Techniques, and also to celebrate the success of Volume 1 by publishing this 2nd edition, complete with new, modern-look, cover design, and 8 dynamic action photos for pulling out and framing, while retaining the much-praised *Wai Khru Ram Muay* poster. As always, we welcome feedback from our readers, and would particularly like to know what *you* would like to see covered in Vol.2. Please send your suggestions/comments by e-mail to us at (feedback@sprypublishing.com)

Kat Prayukvong
Lesley D. Junlakan
1 February 2005
Bangkok, Thailand

CHAPTER 1

The History and Development of Muay

With a lack of written records and an oral traditon which has been highly embellished by legends and stories, the pre-20th century history of *muay* is hard to plot with any degree of certainty. This chapter provides as accurate a picture as it is possible to form of the origins of *muay* and its development down the centuries.

The "History at a Glance" section makes it easy to set these developments in the context of Thai history in general. In order to distinguish between the old and modern forms of this martial art, "Muay Thai" is used only of the post-1920s era, after the introduction of gloves and other elements of Western boxing, while "*muay*" is used to refer to the original concept, modified as necessary by the addition of other terms: *Muay Kaad Chuek, Muay Luang, Muay Boran* and so on.

The
Legend
of Shaolin Temple

There is a legend, believed implicitly by some, rejected categorically by others, that most, if not all, of the great martial arts of the Orient can trace their origins to Shaolin Temple in China. The first abbot of the temple, so the story goes, was Takmor, an Indian prince, who, like Buddha himself, had renounced worldly wealth to devote himself to religion. Following Takmor's teachings, the Chinese Buddhist monks of Shaolin trained with equal rigor in the arts of meditation and self-defense, on the premise that a strong body leads to a strong spirit. Practically speaking, they also needed to be proficient in the martial arts in order to protect themselves when they retreated into the forest to meditate, to defend their temple from marauders and to guard their brothers engaged in the painstaking process of copying holy manuscripts.

If this legend is true, then it can be endlessly speculated how, spreading from their common origins in Shaolin Temple to the surrounding countries, martial arts as diverse as taekwondo (Korea), karate (Japan) and possibly the Muay Thai prototype developed in their own unique ways, while maintaining the integral elements of meditation and the calming of the spirit as evidence of their religious beginnings.

The Origins of
Muay

(M u a y - มวย)

The precise origins of the martial art which is known today as Muay Thai are hazy and imprecise. Very little written documentation exists that provides a factual and accurate picture of how and in what ways it developed down the centuries, while the oral tradition has been embellished by legends and hearsay to the extent that it is now difficult to distinguish fact from fiction. Even the derivation of the term *muay* itself is unclear. According to one school of thought, it comes from the Sanskrit *mavya*, meaning "to pull together", as in pulling hair into a pony-tail, "to form into a single group or unit", or "unity". Although this theory cannot be dismissed out of hand, it is, surely, rather too glib deduce from this, as some have done, that the word can be directly linked to the "pulling together" or "binding" which is an important aspect of four elements in *muay*: the head in the *mongkon*; the biceps in the *prajied;* the fists in the *kaad chuek;* and the spirit through the uttering of incantations.

Undoubtedly *muay* originated as a practical fighting skill, using parts of the body itself -- the head, fists, elbows, knees and feet -- with or without additional weaponry such as swords, pikes and staffs. It was used both on the battlefield itself, at the time when hand-to-hand combat was the norm, and to protect the community against marauders. This form of fighting must have developed concurrently throughout most of the Indochina Peninsula and not in isolation in the area covered by modern-day Thailand. In the frequent aggressive encounters between the forces of the various kingdoms which existed in centuries past, the fighters would have had chances to observe the techniques which were being used by their

adversaries and then incorporate them into their own arsenal. This can be substantiated by the fact that alongside modern-day Muay Thai, less celebrated but equally valid derivative forms of *muay* are practiced throughout the South-East Asian region. Even to this day, an annual Muay Laos contest is held in Nong Khai near the north-eastern border with Laos, on the Thai side of the Maekong River, while a Muay Burma contest is staged in the Maesord district of Tak Prefecture, western Thailand, during the Songkran festivities which mark the Thai New Year (13th April).

It can be speculated with a fair degree of certainty that the link between *muay* and local temples is almost as old as *muay* itself. When Buddhism spread into the region from its birthplace in India, it was readily embraced by the local inhabitants. The temple (*wat*), with its community of monks, many of whom were retired soldiers and high-ranking officials or members of the nobility, educated men who had been successful in their secular lives, was very much at the center of each village, both literally and figuratively speaking. The local people sent their sons to live and study a broad range of subjects with the monks, while the temple itself, with its extensive compound, was the social focus of the neighborhood, the place where people went to pray and to meet each other, and where traditional celebrations and fairs were held. Temples were also power houses for the arts -- not only religious art but the whole spectrum of artistic endeavor, including the martial art of *muay*. It was from the monks, with their knowledge of military strategy and socio-psychology, that young boys and men studied this art of close-quarter combat.

History
at a Glance

Pre-Sukhothai Era c.200 BC-1238

In the 2nd or 3rd centuries BC, Indian Buddhist missionaries were reputedly sent to a land known as Suvarnabhumi, "The Land of Gold", a fertile region stretching, in modern-day terms, from southern Burma, across central Thailand to eastern Cambodia. This region became the center of the Dvaravati culture, which declined under the influence of the invading Khmers in the 11th century, while in the south, Chaiya was the local capital of the Srivijaya empire, based in Sumatra. Meanwhile, a prototype Thai state called Nan Chao was flourishing in what is now south-eastern China. At some point, the people of this state started migrating slowly southwards down the Indochina Peninsula. Some of them became mercenaries in the Khmer armies, where they were referred to as "Syams" from the Sanskrit *syam*, meaning "dark", a reference to their relatively darker skin tones. The name Syam or Siam was eventually used to denote their kingdom.

Muay: Key Points: Spreading throughout the Indochina Peninsula, possibly in conjunction with Buddhism, as a combat skill

Sukhothai Era 1238-1377

In the central northern region of modern-day Thailand, the establishment of Sukhothai as the capital can, in many respects, be regarded as the birth of the prototype Thai nation itself. Founded as the great Khmer empire, which had held sway for about a thousand years, went into decline, the Sukhothai era saw a great flowering of religious art. Many experts maintain that the statues of Buddha produced during this period have never since been surpassed in terms of their purity of line, grace and spirituality. It was also during this era that Ramkamhaeng, arguably the first great Siamese king, codified the country's writing system.

Muay: Functions:	Combat skill on the battlefield
	Defense of the community
	Martial training in peace-time
Key Point:	Fighters bare-fisted

Ayutthaya Era 1350-1767

Just 76 km. (about 50 miles) north of Bangkok, Phra Nakorn Sri Ayutthaya, to give the city its full name, was the capital of the country for over 400 years, from its foundation in 1350 by King U-Thong, to its total destruction by the Burmese in 1767. It became an extremely prosperous city, thriving on trade, and many foreign envoys -- including those from Europe -- were sent there to court the favor of the monarch and to secure trading rights. In its hey-day, Ayutthaya's population and grandeur were both reputed to have exceeded those of London, and with its golden pagodas and great architectural wealth, it must have been a city beyond compare.

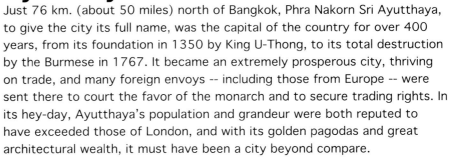

The Ayutthaya period provided Thai history with many heroes -- like King Naresuan who, in 1592, defeated the Burmese crown prince in single-handed, elephant-back combat -- and at least one heroin: Queen Suriyothai, who was mortally wounded in 1548 when, disguised as a warrior, she tried to aid her husband on the battlefield.

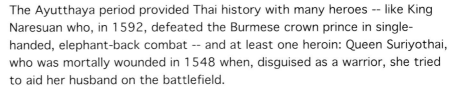

Muay: Functions:	Combat skill in successive wars with Burma
	Defense of the community
	Means of personal advancement
	Training for royalty and the elite
	Sport
Key Point:	Introduction of *kaad chuek*
Heroes of the Day:	*Somdet Prachao* Suer (cf. p.50)
	Nai Khanom Tom (cf. p.51)

Thonburi Era 1767-1782

After the fall of Ayutthaya, the new king, *Prachao* Taksin Maharaj, founded his new capital on the west bank of the Chao Phraya River. Of Chinese ancestry himself, Taksin promoted links with China.

Muay: Functions: Combat skill on the battlefield
                          Defense of the community
                          Means of personal advancement
                          Training for royalty and the elite
                          Sport

Hero of the Day: *Praya* Pi-chai Dab Hak (cf. p.52)

Early Rattanakosin Era 1782-1868

When the Thonburi Period ended, King Putta Yodfah (Rama I) ascended to the throne as the first king of the Chakri dynasty, and he established a new capital for the country on 21st April 1782. This was originally known as Krung Rattanakosin, but the name was later changed to Krungthepmahanakorn. It is internationally known as Bangkok.

Muay: Functions: Military skill
                          Means of personal advancement
                          Training for royalty and the elite
                          Sport

Key Point: Lack of innovation

Hero of the Day: *Muen* Plaan (cf. p.53)

Mid-Rattanakosin Era 1868-1925

The country developed rapidly under Rama V and Rama VI with the expansion of the road network and the introduction of railways. Many Western-based reforms were introduced although, while losing some territory to French Laos and British Burma, Siam itself resisted colonialization.

Muay: Functions: Military training
Self-defense
Exercise and recreation
Means of personal advancement
Key Points: *Muay* boom
First permanent arena (Suan Gularb)
Heroes of the Day: *Pra* Chai Choke Shok Channa
Muen Cha-ngad Choeng Shok
Muen Muay Mee Chue
Muen Mue Maen Mud (cf.pp.30-37)

1925 to The Present

Rocked between military dictatorships and democratic movements by a series of coups d'etat, the country, which became officially known as Thailand in 1949, developed a constitutional monarchy, with King Bhumipol (Rama IX) now on the throne as the world's longest reigning monarch.

Muay: Functions: Professional and amateur sport
Fitness program
Self-defence
Key Points: Introduction of gloves
Standardization of regulations
Building of Ratchadamnoen and
Lumpini Stadiums
Preservation of traditional form, *Muay Boran*
Popularity spreads overseas

Early Muay Contests

At some unspecified point in time, *muay* took a very large and important step along the road which would eventually lead to Muay Thai: as well as continuing to function as a practical fighting technique for use in actual warfare or to protect the community, it became a sport in which the exponents fought in front of spectators who went to watch for entertainment. This kind of *muay* contest gradually became an integral part of local festivals and celebrations, especially those held at temples.

This early competitive form of *muay*, which became known as *Dhee Muay* or *Dhoi Muay*, was a very different spectacle indeed to the Muay Thai of the present. The bare-fisted fighters did not practice any kinds of grasping or grappling tactics. They hovered with dance-like steps, waiting for a chance to move in and attack their opponent, then, quickly withdrew again to wait for the next opportunity. This method has sometimes been likened to the techniques used by *pla gut*, fighting fish. There was no attempt to pair opponents on the basis of weight or size: an expressed willingness to be matched against each other was all that was required. Later, a visual assessment of a prospective pairing was introduced to try to establish some kind of weight parity. Sometimes, a fighter who was having a winning streak was matched against several opponents in succession.

Likewise, there were no real rules in force. It is thought that a fighter who felt bound to lose had the option of conceding defeat before the contest even began, otherwise the fight would simply continue until one person gave in. The "ring" was nothing more than an area of bare earth, around which the spectators clustered, leaving a roughly circular shape, about eight meters across, so that the fighters had space to move freely. A later development was the use of ropes to mark out a square area for fighting. The division of a contest into rounds was eventually introduced but the number of rounds was not defined. The length of each round was determined by placing in water a coconut shell with a hole bored in the bottom. When the water-level inside the shell had risen to the top and the coconut was thus submerged under water, the round ended. The prizes given to the winning fighters were generally commodities rather than money, but occasionally small cash prizes were awarded.

Bound
Fist Muay

(M u a y   K a a d   C h u e k - ม ว ย ค า ด เ ชื อ ก)

At some point in time which now cannot be pinpointed with any degree of accuracy, an important innovation took place: instead of using their bare-fists, the fighters started to bind them for both extra attacking strength and to protect their fingers and wrists from sprains and other injuries. This fist binding, known as *kaad chuek,* was composed of skeins of unrefined hemp threads twisted together into a soft cord the thickness of the little finger. A length of about twenty meters (about twenty-two yards) was sufficient to bind one hand.

The *kaad chuek* was bound around the palm and back of the hand and the wrist, sometimes around the lower forearm and occasionally even up to the elbow. It is believed that rough coils of the same thread were inserted under the *kaad chuek* on the back of the knuckles to form protuberances known as *gon hoi*, or "whorls." There were no specifications as to the permissible or standard number of *gon hoi*: four was probably regarded as the basic minimum, one for each of the lower knuckles of the clenched fist, while some fighters probably had many more. Before a contest, the fighters immersed their bound fists in water: the *gon hoi* then hardened and "welded" with the *kaad chuek* as they dried, becoming capable of inflicting a nasty injury. The use of *kaad chuek* rapidly spread as fighters realized that the bound fist was stronger and tougher than bare hands, providing both offensive advantages and protection against injury.

There is a notorious legend about the *kaad chuek* which maintains that on some occasions the skeins were first soaked in flour and water paste, tree resin, or some other similar sticky substance into which fragments of glass, stone chippings, or other abrasive materials had been mixed. The saturated skeins were then dried in the sun, so that the abrasive materials became firmly embedded within them. If this is true, undoubtedly the treated *kaad chuek* would have had even greater offensive potential, and could have caused very severe injuries indeed.

Inevitably, there is no consensus as to how and when the *kaad chuek* were used. One theory is that the *kaad chuek* were used for contests only and not for actual combat as they would have made the fists rather stiff and clumsy, incapable of holding and wielding weaponry with any accuracy. Another possibility is that soldiers were divided into two ranks: those who had their fists bound in *kaad chuek* and whose duty was to use *muay* techniques alone against their adversaries, and another contingent whose fists were not bound and who used swords and other weapons on the battlefield. The theory that the *kaad chuek* were actually used to bind a weapon onto the fighter's hand also has its supporters, as does a yet another speculation which makes a distinction between ordinary, untreated *kaad chuek* for competitive use and the treated *kaad chuek* which were reserved for warfare.

Early
Training
Methods

In those early days of *muay*, it goes without saying that there was no specific equipment for training: fighters used whatever they could find or devise in the tropical environment to help them develop the appropriate skills and physique. For example, the smooth trunk of the banana tree was an early form of punch-bag, being used for the whole range of target practice with the fists, elbows, knees and feet, while climbing coconut trees helped to develop power in the arms and legs, especially the knees. The legs were also strengthened by running in rivers or lakes or by jumping in and out of a waist-deep pit. It is thought that fighters toughened their shins by pressing and rolling small logs up and down the front of their legs. The power and accuracy of punches was increased by using floating coconuts as targets. Eye-sight was enhanced by using a lime suspended on a vine or creeper for punching and avoidance practice.

Royal Muay

(M u a y L u a n g - มวยหลวง)

Muay gradually became a possible means of personal advancement as the nobility increasingly esteemed skillful practitioners of the art and invited selected fighters to come and live in the palace to teach *muay* to the staff of the royal household, soldiers, princes or the king's personal guards.

It is known that at some stage during the Ayutthaya Period, a platoon of royal guards, whose duty was to protect king and country, variously known as the *Gong Tanai Luak* (Elite Retainers), *Dhamruot Luang* (Royal Police) or *Grom Nak Muay* (*Muay* Fighters' Regiment) was established. Officers in the force were highly skilled in the art of *muay*; indeed they had attained this rank by personal selection after having exhibited exceptional skills and techniques while fighting in front of the monarch himself. This elite form of *muay*, in which fighters became honored guards who also taught the princes and other members of the nobility, became known as *Muay Luang* or Royal *Muay*.

This royal patronage of *muay* and the system of promoting the most skillful fighters to the ranks of the *Gong Tanai Luak* continued right through to the reigns of Rama V and VI, when fighters who had proved themselves through a succession of bouts in the provinces were invited to go to the capital and fight in a spectacle attended by the king himself or his representative.

The Muay
Renaissance

Rama V & Rama VI (1868 - 1925)

The accession of King Chulalongkorn (Rama V) to the throne in 1868 ushered in a Golden Age not only for *muay* but for the country as a whole as, with his inquiring mind and broad outlook, he set his nation on the road to becoming a modern society. Not for nothing is he one of the most revered Thai monarchs.

Muay progressed greatly during the reign of King Chulalongkorn as a direct result of the king's personal interest in the art. The country was at peace, so *muay* functioned as a means of physical exercise, self-defense, recreation...and personal advancement. Four fighters in particular achieved fame and honor through the personal favor of King Chulalongkorn, prompting a *muay* boom which laid the foundations for the future development of the art.

The first of these was an exponent of *Muay Pra Nakorn* (Bangkok-style *muay*) who impressed the king greatly when he saw him fight. He was given the splendid title *Pra* Chai Choke Shok Channa (Lord Lucky-Fight-and Win) and went on to become a very famous teacher of both *muay* and *krabi krabong*.

The three other fighters achieved rank and honor simultaneously on an occasion with which *muay* might not be readily associated: a funeral. In 1898, Marupongsiripat, a high-ranking army commander, passed away, and, as part of the royally-sponsored funeral rites, many *muay* fighters from all over the country were invited to come and show their skills in the presence of King Chulalongkorn at the Grand Palace. The king really enjoyed the spectacle and was particularly impressed by these three fighters, all practitioners of different regional forms of *muay*. He promoted them to high-ranking military officers and himself devised their honorary names -- all of which have a suitably propitious meaning:

> *Muen* Cha-ngad Choeng Shok - Knight of the Clear-Fighting-Tactic
> *Muen* Muay Mee Chue - Knight of the Famous-*Muay*
> *Muen* Mue Maen Mud - Knight of the Punch-and-Strike-Hand

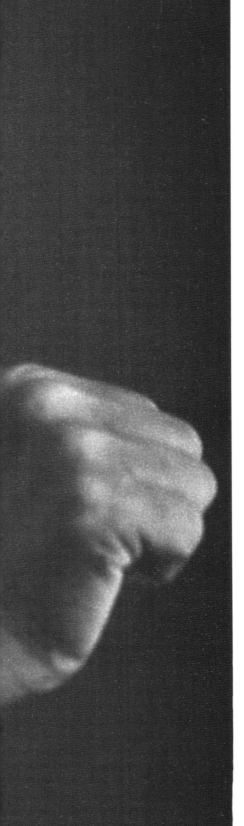

Muay
Chaiya

(M u a y   C h a i y a - มวยไชยา)

Historical Context
One of the three main cities of the Srivijaya Kingdom

Present Day
Market town in Surat-thani Province, southern Thailand, famed for its
Salty Ducks Eggs

In Brief
Characteristic
Referred to as *Muay giow*, because, just like the teasing interplay of
courtship, it uses the brain to decide on strategy and tactics

Distinctive Points

The body is held in an angular manner, like the spines on a durian, the King of Fruit. This makes it difficult to attack as the aggressor can be easily hurt on any of the points.

Muay Chaiya Stance

Angular, with elbows and knees bent, feet well apart. In the *Muay Chaiya* style *Yaang Sam Khum,* the preparatory stance is maintained throughout, creating a very angular effect. The protective forearm becomes in itself a passive weapon as it obstructs the attacking opponent and inflicts pain on them.

Fist Binding

Bound thickly but only down to the wrist. It is believed that the old form of *Muay Chaiya* used to flick the wrist, using the back of the hand to deftly hit away an on-coming blow

Special Technique

*Suer Larg Hang (*The Tiger Pulls the Tail), the technique used by *Muen* Muay Mee Chue to secure victory when fighting in front of Rama V. To execute this deceptive move, the fighter crouches down low, one leg stretched out behind him with the knee and toes on the floor. The opponent, assuming he has the advantage, raises his leg to kick, but as he does so, the fighter reaches in, grasps the supporting leg and pulls it from under him.

Muay Chaiya Teachers

Paw-Tan Mar was an itinerant monk who became the abbot of a temple in the village of Pum Riang, Chaiya, in the mid-nineteenth century. Renowned as a great teacher, legend has it that he once used hollow coconuts to catch an elephant which was devastating the grounds of his temple. This feat gave the temple the name by which it is known today: *Wat* Tung-Jap-Charng or The Elephant-Caught-in-the-Field Temple. Nowadays, the temple is in ruins, but the *chedi*, or pagoda, in which the bones of the abbot were deposited, remains. Local people still go there to "consult" with his spirit, offering a small model elephant if their wishes are granted.

Praya (Count) Watjeesattayarak, the local ruler of Chaiya, who was the teacher of *Muen* Muay Mee Chue

Muen (Knight) Muay Mee Chue, who brought honor and prestige to *Muay Chaiya*

Nin Paksee, a contemporary of *Muen* Muay Mee Chue, who was extremely skillful and never lost a bout. However, as he was handicapped, with a deformed leg, it was thought inappropriate for him to go up to Bangkok to fight in front of the king. Therefore he lost the chance of winning fame and fortune.

Khru Kaet Sriyapai, the son of *Praya* Watjeesattayarak, studied under no less than 13 *khru muay* before becoming a great teacher himself. Towards the end of his life he is reputed to have said:

I have studied muay since I was 10 until I've reached the age of 70, and I've still got plenty to learn. So if someone says 'I am skillful, I know everything,' I believe that person can never reach the heart of muay.

Khru Tong Yaleh, a student of *Khru* Kaet. With him, the great era of *Muay Chaiya* came to an end.

Khru Kaet

Khru Tong

The First Permanent Arena

Muay retained its immense popularity in the reign of King Wajirawudh (Rama VI), 1910 - 1925, who himself traveled to many places, including Korat, Chumporn and Nakorn Sri-Tammarat, to watch specially arranged Royal *Muay* contests. It was while Wajirawudh was king that in 1920 *muay* contests finally got their first permanent home, Suan Gularb Arena. (For further details of this and other arenas and stadiums, cf. pp.54-59)

In the following year, a fight between Yang Harn Talay, an exponent of *Muay Korat,* and a Chinese fighter called Jee Chang was staged at the arena. People were extremely interested in this epoch-making event so tickets for the bout were quickly sold out to both Chinese and Siamese supporters, and spectators were seated several hours before the fight was due to commence. Yang Harn Talay won by a knock-out after he followed a punch to the face with a powerful kick to the neck. Jee Chang lay motionless on the ground and was still unable to get to his feet by the time the referee had counted to ten.

From Thailand to the World

Rama VII (1925) - Present Day

Even as late as the 1920s, *kaad chuek* was still in use in the ring. However, in 1926 the death knell for this ancient *muay* tradition, at least as far as the standard form of the art was concerned, was sounded when one fighter, Jia Kaegkhmen, died in the ring of the Lak Muang Arena after being punched by Pae Lieng Prasert. Jia clung to the ropes dying but refusing to

give in, so the referee could not technically count him out: it can be speculated, therefore, that the lack of clear regulations governing *muay* was responsible for his tragic death as much as anything else. After this, a new rule was introduced stating that fighters should wear gloves and, rather oddly, also socks. To all intents and purposes, Muay Thai had been born.

The first fighters to fight at Lak Muang Arena wearing gloves and socks were Kammuey Muang Yod and Nop Chom Sri Maek. Both of them stumbled and slipped in the ring because of their unfamiliarity with the socks, turning the bout into something of a fiasco. The spectators were acutely dissatisfied by the contest and so, although the use of gloves was continued, the wearing of socks was abandoned. However, the change-over from *kaad chuek* to gloves was not instantaneous: there are references to *kaad chuek* still being used in mainstream bouts well into the 1930s, indicating that it took about a decade for their use to be phased out.

It was in 1928 that a very rudimentary ranking system for Muay Thai was first implemented, the title fight to decide who was *Yod Muay Aek* -- the number one fighter -- being held on 15th November that year. People flocked to see the fight and the even greater popularity of Muay Thai paved the way to the siting of yet more arenas. However, it was not until 1950 that a fully-developed ranking system with 8 weight-divisions calculated in pounds, was finally implemented with the assistance of Major General Sullivan, an American G.I. stationed in the Philippines.

In 1929, "the box" or groin protector (*gra-jap*), then made from metal, was used in Siam for the first time. It was introduced into the country by Aer Muong Dee who had seen it while fighting in Singapore. Other Muay Thai fighters were impressed by its convenience and safety, so its use became widespread, extending down to the present day.

Throughout the late-twenties and thirties, Muay Thai training was progressively developed. Gymnasiums were constructed, body and muscle-building exercises were devised, punch-bags and punch-balls became widely available, and the use of training gloves and contest gloves became the norm. Facilities at Muay Thai training camps were also standardized.

During World War II, the people's interest in Muay Thai did not wane, and contests were still held either in actual arenas, or in converted movie theaters such as Sri Aytthuya, Pattanagorn and Wong Wien Yai.

Since World War II, Muay Thai has been subject to changing fortunes. Various entrepreneurs arranged for Muay Thai fighters to go to America and other countries to stage exhibition bouts or to match their Muay Thai skills against exponents of other martial arts, such as karate and Western boxing.

In the late 1950s, Osamu Noguchi, a Japanese entrepreneur in the field of Western-style boxing, became extremely interested in Muay Thai. He filmed Muay Thai fighters in action in Thailand and screened it back in Japan for the benefit of himself and his students. It was in the years immediately following on from this that he devised the concept of kick-boxing, a martial art which fuses Muay Thai's kicking techniques, with aspects of karate and, to some degree, Western-style boxing. In 1964, he was back in Thailand with a troupe of his Japanese kick-boxers for a contest against Muay Thai fighters. Later, he introduced this sport into Europe, thus originating the common error among many Westerners that Muay Thai and kick-boxing are synonymous, or even that Muay Thai developed from kick-boxing.

In Thailand itself, Muay Thai flourished in the 1970s, a decade which, in the opinion of many, saw the emergence of a host of young fighters whose skills, grace and mastery of the refined *Mae Mai Muay Thai* techniques will never be surpassed. It was in the same decade that, thanks to the movies of the kung-fu king, Bruce Lee, the oriental martial arts in general enjoyed a boom, especially in the USA, where people flocked to acquire the skills for themselves. Muay Thai also rode on the crest of this wave and Muay Thai gyms opened across the country. It also became popular in many European countries, especially Germany and Holland, and Australia.

Ancient
Muay

(Muay Boran - มวยโบราณ)

It was, perhaps, inevitable that while Muay Thai became standardized and internationalized, absorbing many elements of Western boxing, there were those who looked back fondly to the old days of *kaad chuek*. *Muay Boran* (Ancient Muay) is the term now used to refer to the practice of this bygone form of *muay*, which, for its devotees, is a much purer, more traditional form of the art. *Muay Boran* is still taught in Thailand: training is a very long and involved process, for whereas, generally speaking, a Muay Thai teacher instructs his students in the rudimentary techniques with a view to enabling them to enter the ring as soon as possible, the *Muay Boran* instructor stresses traditional aspects and methods, not progressing from one technique to another until he is completely satisfied that the students fully comprehend all it entails, not least the aesthetic and ritual elements. It has been said, with more than a little truth, that *Muay Boran* students will have to practice walking techniques for a month before they are allowed to progress to the next step.

Without a doubt, the *Yaang Sam Khum* (The Muay Shuffle) is at the heart of *Muay Boran*. It is known in *Muay Boran* circles as *Tar Khru* (The Teacher's Form) because it is so permeated by the teacher's own methods and techniques that by watching fighters execute the *Yaang Sam Khum* alone, it is possible to deduce whose students they are. At the conclusion of the *Wai Khru Ram Muay,* which is a very extended ritual in *Muay Boran,* fighters walk protractedly in the *Yaang Sam Khum,* revealing, as they do so, their own inherent strengths and weaknesses.

Muay Boran very much follows the precedents of its ancient predecessor in that very few actual regulations apply: all parts of the body are potential targets and some techniques are capable of inflicting severe injuries in the hands of a master. Pairings for bouts are also done in the old style, being decided by the mutual agreement of those concerned rather than by following any weight-divisions. It remains a very beautiful, highly ritualized form of *muay*, yet is both extremely effective if faced with a real-life assault and entertaining to watch in the ring.

Towards the
Future

A new challenge faces Muay Thai as it jostles to become an Olympic or a South-East Asian Games event. To comply with the ruling that the title of an Olympic sport cannot incorporate the name of any country, it would be necessary for Muay Thai to change its name. Inevitably, there would also be signs of dissent from Laos, Cambodia and Burma over the disputed "ownership" of this martial art.

Today, men and women of all ages, races and religions appreciate that Muay Thai is an extremely effective form of exercise and self-defense, easily on a par with other international martial arts, and enjoy regular training sessions. As a professional sport, regulated by the same standards world-wide, its popularity has spread across the globe with world championships comparable to those for Western boxing now being held. In addition, Muay Thai has become an accepted amateur sport in more than one hundred countries. Muay Thai, the one-time favored military art of kings, is now, indeed, a king among martial arts.

Gallery of Legendary Muay Heroes

Somdet Prachao Suer

The 29th king of the Ayutthaya period, *Somdet Prachao* Suer (otherwise known as King Sri Sanpetch VIII) was highly respected for his *muay* skills and knowledge. In his youth, the prince, then known as *Khun Luang* Sorrasak, used to practice *muay* in the palace, later traveling from one place to another as a student of the martial art, until he became a highly-skilled practitioner himself.

One apocryphal story relates how, in 1702, the forty-two-year-old king, hearing that there was to be a *muay* contest at a temple fair in Barn Pajanta, Wiset Chaichan township, set off from the palace with a small entourage. Disguising himself as a peasant so that he could take part incognito, he sent a messenger to ask the promoter if any fighter was prepared to be matched against a *nak muay* from the city. The best local fighter came forwards and fought with the king, but he was soon injured and eventually defeated. As a prize, the king was given one *baht*. The king expressed his willingness to fight again, and emerged the victor in several more bouts before returning to the palace with the personal satisfaction of having fought and won. All those who had seen the fights went back to their homes suitably impressed by the *muay* skills of the unknown stranger from the city.

So great was his love of *muay*, that, in addition to such escapades, *Somdet Prachao* Suer seriously encouraged people throughout the kingdom to study and train in *muay* and actively promoted *muay* contests at local fairs and festivals. He also gave his personal support to *muay* training programs in the royal palace itself. The name of *Somdet Prachao* Suer, "The Tiger King," does indeed deserve a special place in the annals of *muay*

Nai Khanom Tom

After the Burmese besieged and finally overran Ayutthaya in 1767, they rounded up many of their Siamese captives and took them back to Burma as prisoners of war. Among them was a skillful *muay* fighter called *Nai* Khanom Tom.

Time passed and, in 1774, King Mangra of Burma went to Rangoon to attend a celebration at Ket Tat Pagoda. Various kinds of entertainment were staged and the king decided to try to prove which martial art was the superior: *muay* Siam or *muay* Burma. Among the captives from Ayutthaya chosen to take part in the bouts was *Nai* Khanom Tom.

The Burmese form of *muay* predominantly used the fists and the fighters wore traditional ankle-length sarongs, restricting their leg movements. On the other hand, Siamese *muay,* as has already been seen, used not only the fists but also elbows, knees and feet and the fighters wore *paa-nung* with their hands bound in the *kaad chuek*.

Nai Khanom Tom defeated several Burmese fighters in succession. King Mangra praised him, declaring, "Every part of this man is blessed with venom. Even empty-handed, he could defeat nine or ten opponents".

Nai Khanom Tom is commemorated by a statue in Ayutthaya's Provincial Sports Ground. Around the base are four sparring pairs, showing the use of the fist, elbow, knee and foot, while a plaque records the legend in brief:

> *Khanom Tom, a citizen of the Ancient City of Ayutthaya, was a war captive brought to Myanmar after the city s fall in 1767. During one special occasion to celebrate the erection of an umbrella over a great stupa, Khanom Tom was summoned to perform an exhibition bout in Thai boxing before the King of Ava. Legend relates that at that special event, Khanom Tom, with his boxing prowess, defeated ten opponents in succession on that same day.*

17th March, the day on which, according to tradition, *Nai* Khanom Tom, the "Father of Muay Thai", fought against the Burmese, eventually became recognized as "Muay Thai Day".

Praya Pi-chai Dab Hak

Born in the late Ayutthaya Period, Joi was the son of poor rice farmers. His father gave him to a temple in Pi-chai, where he was raised by monks from whom he learnt the art of *muay*.

One day, Joi got involved in a fight with the son of the local lord. Afraid that his parents and the monks would blame him for his rashness, he ran away and changed his name to Tong Dee Fan Khao, hoping that no-one would be able to follow him. He followed an itinerant life-style, training in *muay* here and there. Going to see a Chinese drama, he was greatly impressed by the mid-air maneuvers performed by the troupe and begged them to teach him their techniques. Some time after this, he met *Khru* Maek, who arranged for him to fight at a fair where his leaping skills earned him victory.

On the advice of *Khru* Maek, who thought Tong Dee should train in other martial arts and secure a better life for himself by becoming a soldier, he went to study swordsmanship in Suwangalok.

Later, Tong Dee met a Chinese merchant in Sukhothai. He was on his way to Tak and was afraid of the tiger-infested jungle which lay ahead of him. He told Tong Dee that he should become a soldier in the army of *Praya* Tak, and suggested that they travel together. Tong Dee accepted the proposal and they set off along with Tong Dee's pupil, Bungirt. The merchant's fears were sadly justified: Bungirt was mauled and killed by a tiger, which Tong Dee then killed in revenge.

Arriving in Tak, Tong Dee went to fight in a tournament arranged by *Praya* Tak, and won all his bouts. *Praya* Tak was impressed and not only invited Tong Dee to become one of his guards, but made him lord of Kampaeng-pet, a neighboring town.

Shortly after this, the Burmese invaded, so *Praya* Tak and *Praya* Kampaeng-phet, as Tong Dee was now known, went into battle. One of *Praya* Kampaeng-pet's adversaries was the Burmese general Ney-mio-see-ha-ba-dee: although his sword was broken in the fierce combat, he nevertheless slayed the general.

After the fall of Ayutthaya, *Praya* Tak became *Prachao* Taksin *Maharaj*, king of his newly-founded capital of Thonburi. *Praya* Kampaeng-phet was appointed lord of the town where he had been brought up and, to this day, he is celebrated as "*Praya* Pi-chai Dab Hak", or "Count Pi-chai with the Broken Sword".

* See Appendix A for map showing all these places

Muen Plaan

In 1788, at the beginning of the reign of Rama I, two French brothers came to Siam to challenge the local *muay* fighters, having already fought and won against many types of boxers across the Indochina Peninsula. The Keeper of the Treasury conveyed their message to the king, who consulted with his brother on the matter. They felt that it was a matter of national pride that the Siamese fighter should win, so, after much discussion, a member of the Royal Guards, highly skilled in *muay*, was selected to take up the challenge. The bout was staged in the grounds of The Grand Palace and was watched by the king himself.

When the fight began, the younger of the two French brothers, with his powerful physique, immediately went on the offensive against his opponent. The royal guardsman struck out defensively with his fists and feet, preventing the Frenchman from coming too close to him. As the contest progressed, the guardsman's constant defensive kicks and punches put the Frenchman at a disadvantage. The older brother then jumped into the ring to try to put an end to the *muay* fighter's continual backing and avoiding tactics, after which the bout disintegrated into a free-for-all as his comrades in the Royal Guards jumped into the ring to help him. The two French brothers suffered many injuries so the king ordered them to be taken care of and their wounds attended to. The French contingent went back to their ship and set sail the next day, never daring to challenge a Siamese fighter again.

It was, presumably, after this rather strange encounter that the guardsman was given an honorary rank and name by King Rama I: *Muen* Plaan, meaning "Knight of Destruction".

Muay
Arenas
& Stadiums

Even though the history of *muay* arenas and stadiums commences within living memory, there is a notable lack of, or only very imprecise, documentation relating to the pre-Ratchadamnoen days. It is, therefore, impossible to give precise facts and figures for the early arenas, especially when they came into and fell out of use. Except for some specific dates, therefore, generalizations only are given below. Map references (see p.57) for all the arenas and stadiums are given.

The Age of Arenas

The very first permanent locations for the presentation of *muay* contests were very modest affairs indeed: no buildings or other facilities, just an area of land, as their Thai name, *sanam muay* (*muay* field) indicates.

Suan Gularb Arena

In use: From 1920 for about 10 years
Location: Saipet Road, near Pahurat Market
Nowadays: In the grounds of Suan Gularb School

Suan Gularb Arena was the first permanent home for the staging of *muay* contests. Some years previously, Rama V had given a piece of temple land for the founding of Suan Gularb School. It was his successor's decision to arrange for the area enclosed by the school's classic arcades to be used for *muay* contests every Saturday. Initially, bouts took place on the bare earth, the large field-cum-ring, which measured 20 meters by 20 meters (about 21.5 yards by 21.5 yards), being delineated by a line marked on the ground. The spectators gathered around the ring, which they were officially not allowed to enter. However, a problem arose when, on one occasion, the spectators invaded the fighting area. This led to the arena's ruling committee's decision to introduce a raised ring, constructed about 120cm. (about 4 feet) above the ground, marked out by two parallel ropes, with mats on the floor and steps leading up to it.

Indicative, no doubt, of the arena's royal patronage, the referee initially wore rich silk Thai pantaloons, white socks and official-style white jacket. This was later changed to a military combat style. Many details of the format of the bouts which took place there have been lost but the following generalizations can be made:

a. whereas previously the referee had stood outside the ring, he was now positioned inside
b. the referee observed the fight and had powers to intervene when necessary
c. the number of rounds was fixed in advance
d. a weight-parity system was still not in use: the mutual agreement of both parties was the all-important factor
e. *kaad chuek* were still in use

Tar Charng Arena B
Location: By the river near Tar Charng
Nowadays: The Naval Welfare Department

Lak Muang Arena C
Location: Lak Muang Road
Nowadays: Dept. of Public Prosecutors, behind the City Pillar

Suan Sanuk Arena D
In use: From 9th November 1929 through the 1930s
Location: Rama IV Road/Wireless Road
Nowadays: In vicinity of clock tower, Wireless Road entrance to Lumpini Park

Suan Jao Ched Arena E
In use: Pre-World War II years
Location: Charoen Krung Road/Sanam Chai road
Nowadays: Territorial Defense Department

These four arenas -- and possibly others which went completely unrecorded -- all came and went between the mid-1920s and the late-1930s. They were in use during the transitional period between *kaad chuek* and gloves: interestingly enough, there are records of *kaad chuek* still being in use in the immediate pre-war years at the Suan Jao Ched Arena, indicating just how long it took for the change-over to be complete. With the exception of the Suan Sanuk Arena, they were all clustered in a very small area in the vicinity of the Grand Palace and *Wat* Po, in what today is termed Rattanakosin Island.

Very little is known about the Tar Charng Arena, while Lak Muang Arena's claim to fame is the Jia Kaegkhamen tragedy which led to the introduction of gloves (cf. p.40).

Suan Sanuk -- "Pleasure Garden" -- is slightly better documented. The arena featured an improved, cloth-covered ring which had three ropes around the edge to conform with international standards for Western boxing. The corner colors were also standardized for the first time: red and blue. In addition to the referee inside the ring to control the actual fight, there was also an official to act as a time-keeper and to sound the bell at the end of each round. Another official awarded points and kept track of the score which finally decided who was the winner on points. A contest consisted of either three or six rounds by prior agreement.

The Suan Jao Ched Arena was named after a well-known government official of the day who gave the land for the erection of a ring and the holding of contests, many of which functioned as fund-raising events for the Thai military in the years leading up to World War II.

The War Years

Tar Prachan Arena
Location: Prachan Road
Nowadays: In vicinity of ferry pier and shopping precinct, side of Thammasat University

Pattanagorn Theater G
Location: Charoen Krung Road
Nowadays: The disused Sirirama Cinema in the vicinity of Leng Noy Yee (Mangon) Temple, China Town

Sri Ayutthaya Theater H
Location: Dinsor Road/Bamrungmuang Road,
Nowadays: Residential block near The Giant Swing

Thonburi Theater I
Location: Wong Wien Yai, Thonburi
Nowadays: Wong Wien Yai roundabout, with statue of King Taksin

During the war years, Muay Thai contests continued to be held and were a popular attraction. Very little is known about the Tar Prachan Arena, while the other three were movie theaters which were also used to stage Muay Thai matches.

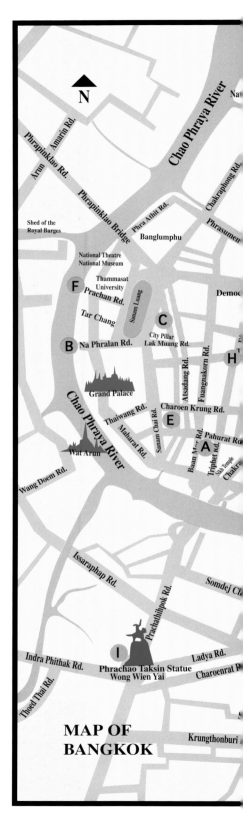

MAP OF
BANGKOK

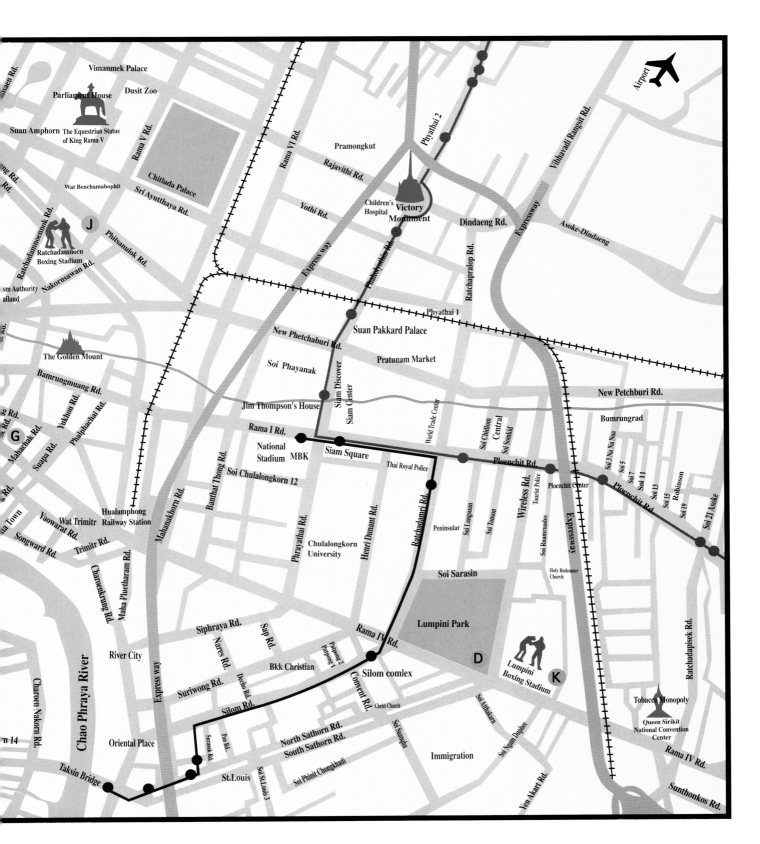

Vimanmek Palace

Parliament House Dusit Zoo

Suan Amphorn The Equestrian Statue of King Rama V

Wat Benchamabophit

Chitlada Palace

Rama V Rd.

Sri Ayutthaya Rd.

Rama VI Rd.

Pramongkut

Rajavithi Rd.

Yothi Rd.

Phyathai 2

Airport

Victory Monument

Children's Hospital

Dindaeng Rd.

Vibhavadi Rangsit Rd.

Asoke-Dindaeng

Expressway

J

Phitsanulok Rd.

Ratchadamnoen Boxing Stadium

Nakornsawan Rd.

sm Authority ailand

Express way

Phyathai 1

Ratchapralop Rd.

Phayathai Rd.

The Golden Mount

Bamrungmuang Rd.

Yukhon Rd.

Phalphachai Rd.

New Phetchaburi Rd.

Suan Pakkard Palace

Pratunam Market

New Petchburi Rd.

Soi Phayanak

Siam Discover

Siam Center

Jim Thompson's House

Bumrungrad

G

Mahachak Rd.

Suapa Rd.

Rama I Rd.

National Stadium MBK

Siam Square

Thai Royal Police

World Trade Center

Soi Chidlom

Central

Soi Somkid

Ploenchit Rd.

Tourist Police

Ploenchit Center

Soi 3 Na Nua

Soi 5

Soi 7

Soi 11

Soi 13

Soi 15

Robinson

Soi 19

Ploenchit Rd.

Soi 21 Asoke

Soi Chulalongkorn 12

Wat Trimitr

Hualamphong Railway Station

Banthat Thong Rd.

Phrayathai Rd.

Henri Dunant Rd.

Ratchadamri Rd.

Peninsular

Soi Langsuan

Soi Tonson

Wireless Rd.

Soi Ruamrudee

Expressway

Yaowarat Rd.

Songward Rd.

Trimitr Rd.

Maha Phuetharam Rd.

Chulalongkorn University

Soi Sarasin

Holy Redeemer Church

Ratchadapisek Rd.

a Town

Charoenkrung Rd.

Mahanakhorn Rd.

Lumpini Park

D

Lumpini Boxing Stadium

K

Chao Phraya River

Siphraya Rd.

River City

Nares Rd.

Sap Rd.

Bkk Christian

Rama IV Rd.

Silom comlex

Convent Rd.

Christ Church

Soi Athakarn

Soi Ngam Duphee

Tobacco Monopoly

Queen Sirikit National Convention Center

Charoen Nakorn Rd.

Suriwong Rd.

Decho Rd.

Patpong 2

Patpong 1

Silom Rd.

Pan Rd.

Surasak Rd.

Oriental Place

Taksin Bridge

St.Louis

Soi St.Louis 3

Soi Phinit Chongkhadi

North Sathorn Rd.

South Sathorn Rd.

Soi Suanplu

Immigration

Yen Akart Rd.

Rama IV Rd.

Sunthonkos Rd.

rn 14

The Post-War Stadiums

Since World War II, Muay Thai has become synonymous with Bangkok's two most famous stadiums, Ratchadamnoen and Lumpini.

Ratchadamnoen Stadium   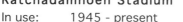 J

In use: 1945 - present
Location: Ratchadamnoen Nok Road

Opened on 23rd December 1945, the original Ratchadamnoen Stadium was an open-air construction, resembling a Roman amphitheater in design. Muay Thai contests were held there every Sunday, commencing at about four or five o'clock in the afternoon. The rules enforced were those which had been formulated by the Department of Physical Education in 1937. It was six years later, in 1951, that a concrete roof was added, making it more convenient and weather-proof. Initially managed by the Crown Property Office, on 24th May 1953 it was privatized as the Ratchadamnoen Co. Ltd.

It has been said that the building of the Ratchadamnoen Stadium marked the final, conclusive steps in the transformation of *muay* from a traditional martial art to a commercial venture. Ticket-holders flocked to see contests there, giving the stadium a good income and this enabled the promoters to pay fighters considerable sums of money for making an appearance. Consequently, there was a sharp increase in the numbers of fighters and Muay Thai training camps, with many fighters turning professional.

Ratchadamnoen Stadium has seen many epoch-making events: for example, a contest there on Saturday, 4th September 1955 became the first ever Muay Thai event to be broadcast on television.

Lumpini Stadium Ⓚ

In use: 8 December 1956 - present
Location: Rama IV Road, near Lumpini Park

Opened more than a decade after Ratchadamnoen, the Lumpini Stadium is run by the military on behalf of the Thai government, the stadium's manager being invariably a high-ranking army official. A friendly rivalry exists between the more glamorous, air-conditioned Ratchadamnoen Stadium, and the more basic, fan-cooled Lumpini, which nevertheless has its own loyal following of spectators.

Muay Thai Contest Information

Ratchadamnoen: Sunday, Monday, Wednesday, Thursday
Lumpini: Tuesday, Friday, Saturday

Time: From around 6pm. - approximately 10pm.
Tickets: Generally in the 200 - 1,000 baht range
Telephone: 02-281-4205 (Ratchadamnoen)
02-251-4303 (Lumpini)

Muay Outfits, Amulets & Incantations

Details of what *muay* fighters wore in the past are very hazy and imprecise. However, it can be deduced that no special clothes were required: they went into the ring wearing the same lower garment as they wore in their everyday lives. Undoubtedly of far greater importance to them than their actual clothes were the amulets (*krueng rang korng klang)* which accompanied them into the ring, bolstered by the utterance of incantations (*kartar arkom). The* fighters believed that such charms had the ability to inspire them with confidence and bravery and to make them invincible, as well as to protect them from the mystical powers likewise invoked by their opponent.

Although modern-day Muay Thai fighters don gloves and satin shorts, and generally speaking belief in such mystic powers has waned, some still have great faith in amulets and incantations, and all fighters are required to wear two kinds of amulets -- *mongkon* and *prajied* -- when they enter the ring.

mongkon

prajied

paa-kao-maa

kaad chuek
(cf.pp.24-25)

The traditional form of the lower garment worn by Thai men can most easily be thought of as being divided into two types a single, unsewn length of cloth (*paa-nung*) and baggy pants (*gung gaeng kaa guay*). With the emphasis on comfort and convenience, these same garments were worn when they took part in *muay* contests.

Paa-Nung (ผ้านุ่ง)

Paa-nung is a generic term for a single, long piece of cloth (*paa*) which is wrapped and tied around the body (*nung*) to form a garment.

In its simplest and earliest form, it was little more than a modest form of loin cloth, as depicted on the *Nai Khanom Tom* monument in Ayutthaya. A more elaborate and later development was *jongrabein*, which involved draping the cloth -- cotton for the average person, silk for the nobility -- to form a pantaloon-style garment which could, incidentally, be worn by either sex. Whatever form the *paa-nung* took, the basic principle was the same: without the use of any seams or additional clips or pins, the cloth was wrapped around the waist, tied, the remaining length twisted, taken backwards between the legs and tucked in at the small of the back.

*gung gaeng
kaa guay*

Traditional
Muay Outfit

Gung Gaeng Kaa Guay (กางเกงขาก๊วย)

Gung gaeng kaa guay, a kind of baggy pants of Chinese origin, were made from cotton. Generally dark blue in color through the use of natural dyes, the legs of the pants reached down to the knee or a little below, while the whole garment was loose, wide, and virtually shapeless, with no waistband, the *paa-kao-maa* being used to secure it around the waist.

Paa-kao-maa (ผ้าขาวม้า)

The *paa-kao-maa* is a much smaller version of *paa-nung,* measuring about 1 meter by 1.5 meters (about 3 ft. by 5 ft.) generally with a checked design. Even today it remains a basic necessity of everyday rural life in Thailand, functioning as a towel, head-cover, belt and so on. In *muay* contests in the early decades of the twentieth century, fighters used at least two *paa-kao-maa,* one for securing the baggy pants at the waist, and one or more for protecting the genitals in the days before the introduction of the groin protector, thickly padding the area between the legs and securely tucking the ends inside the waist *paa-kao-maa.*

Amulets

A wide range of amulets, including the *mongkon* and *prajied* was used by all fighters. For details, refer to pp.68-70

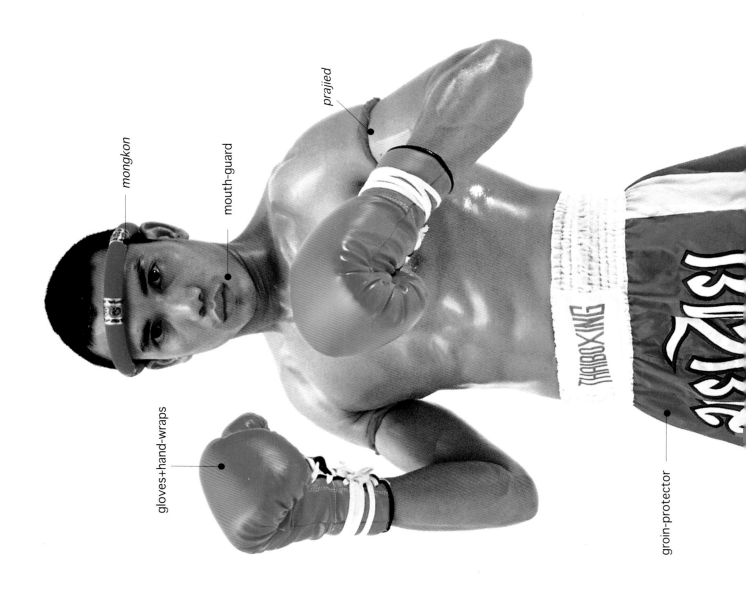

mongkon

mouth-guard

prajied

gloves+hand-wraps

groin-protector

Outfit of
Professiona

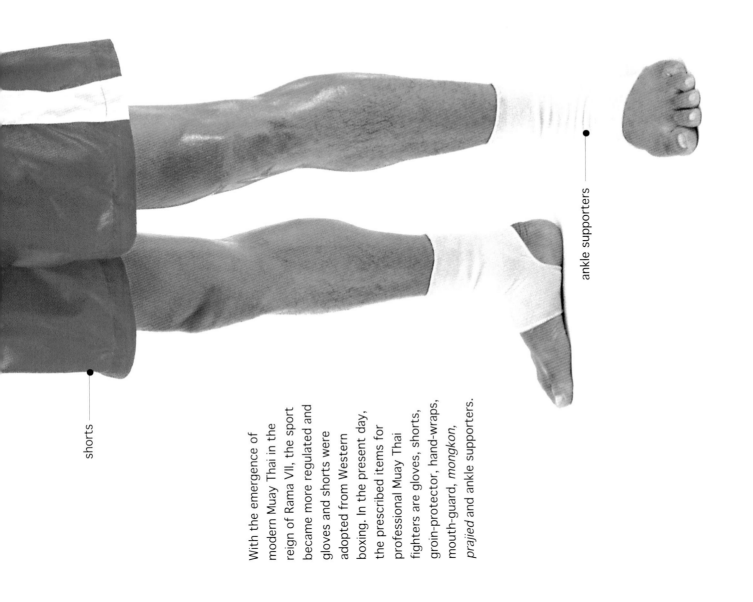

ankle supporters

shorts

With the emergence of modern Muay Thai in the reign of Rama VII, the sport became more regulated and gloves and shorts were adopted from Western boxing. In the present day, the prescribed items for professional Muay Thai fighters are gloves, shorts, groin-protector, hand-wraps, mouth-guard, *mongkon*, *prajied* and ankle supporters.

Muay Thai Fighters Today

head-guard

mouth-guard

vest

prajied

gloves +
Hand-wraps

elbow-guards

body-protector

groin-protector

Outfit of
Amateur

ankle -supporters

shin-guards

shorts

The essential items for amateur Muay Thai fighters nowadays include gloves, vest, shorts, groin-protector, hand-wraps, mouth-guard, *mongkon* (removed after the completion of the *Wai Khru Ram Muay* ritual and replaced by the protective head-guard), *prajied,* ankle -supporters, elbow-guards, body-protector and shin-guards.

Muay Thai Fighters Today

Amulets

(Krueng Rang Korng Klang - เครื่องรางของขลัง)

Amulets have always been an essential part of a *muay* fighter's accouterments. Sacred and highly respected items, when not in use amulets must be kept in a suitably venerated position: if they are put in an inappropriate place, for example on a low shelf or somewhere that people are liable to step over them, it is believed that they will lose their mystical powers. Belief in amulets in the present day is very much a private matter. Fighters not giving credence to them may not even use them at all. However, all Muay Thai fighters must use the *mongkon* and *prajied*. The *mongkon* must be worn until the completion of the *Wai Khru Ram Muay* ritual and then removed before the actual contest, while the *prajied* must be worn throughout. These are matters dictated by tradition in which fighters have no leeway to choose. Other amulets still commonly used are *dhagrut* and *paa-yan* made into *prajied*.

Pra Krueng

Pitsamorn

Pirod

Dhagrut

Prajied

Waahn

Pra Krueng: a small Buddha image secreted inside either the *mongkon* or the *prajied*

Prajied: a band of cloth, traditionally red and white, worn around the upper- arm during a contest to induce toughness and help the fighter to avoid danger. In practice, a Muay Thai fighter can incorporate anything in which he believes and which he venerates into his *prajied* -- or *mongkon* or *pirod*: a strand of his father's hair or even a thread from his mother's *paa-tung* (sarong) used at the time of his birth. As well as the possibility of wearing a *paa-prajied* on one arm and a *gamrai pirod* (q.v.) on the other, other possible variants are to wear a single *prajied* on the more dexterous arm, or to wear a wider band on the more dexterous arm and a narrower band on the less dexterous arm.

Pirod: Fashioned from rattan, the *pirod* takes the form of either a ring -- *wehn pirod* -- or an arm-band -- *gamrai pirod* -- which is worn around the biceps of one arm. It is not customary to wear both the *prajied* and the *pirod* concurrently on the same arm, so an alternative is to wear the *prajied* around one biceps and the *pirod* around the other.

Dhagrut: Consisting of a small sheet of beaten bronze -- or sometimes silver -- inscribed with mystical symbols, the *dhagrut* was rolled up tightly to the accompaniment of incantations, leaving a hole in the center through which, traditionally, a silken thread would be inserted to secure it around the waist. A single *dhagrut* could be worn, in which case it was known as *dhagrut tone*, or several could be threaded together in a variation known as *dhagrut puong*. It was forbidden to ever unfurl a completed *dhagrut* on the assumption that to do so would annul its mystical properties. If very small a *dhagrut* could also be tucked inside the *prajied*.

Pitsamorn: an amulet similar to *dhagrut,* traditionally made from a palm leaf in a woven casing, and tied around the waist.

Waahn: a species of herb which, if used in association with mystic incantations, is believed to endow the fighter with virility and the power to endure the blistering heat of a glancing blow. The fighter either carries the herb inside his *mongkon* or *prajied*, or else actually chews it before and/or during the contest. Some fighters boil the herb or soak it in water, and then either drink the infusion or use it for cleansing their bodies.

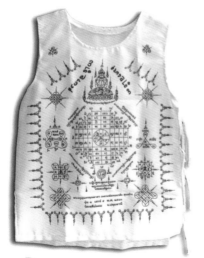

Suea-yan

Suea-yan: cloth made into a waistcoat, which then passes the incantation ritual and is inscribed with unique mystical figures and worn during sacred rites or special ceremonies. In the past, Siamese soldiers also wore such a garment when going into battle.

Mongkon: a circlet worn on the head as a charm to bring prosperity and to protect the wearer from danger. In ancient times, Siamese soldiers tied a type of bandanna around their foreheads before going into battle. It is believed that from this custom arose the tradition of a *khru muay* giving a *mongkon* to his student.

In the distant past, some *muay* training camps or individual teachers developed their own unique methods of making a

Mongkon

mongkon in order to endow it with miraculous powers, including, legend has it, using a live snake -- preferably a poisonous one -- to enhance the effect even more. Supposedly, when the selected snake opened its mouth, its tail was rammed down its own throat, forming it into a circle, in which state it was placed in the sun to die and dry for seven days and nights. The *mongkon* was then woven around this shape. As with the apocryphal story of impregnating the *kaad chuek* with fragments of abrasive material, this is a story which can be neither proved nor disproved, there being no firm evidence.

There was one major difference in the use of the *mongkon* in the past: it was not removed from the fighter's head before the start of the contest. If the *mongkon* fell off during a bout, the opponent stopped his offensive to allow the fighter to replace it: he never used the opportunity to take advantage of his vulnerability.

Paa-yan: a piece of cloth with a unique mystical inscription, sanctified through the utterance of incantations, and then worn by the fighter either as a replacement for or inside the *prajied*.

In addition to the amulets detailed above, some fighters also have a mystical number and/or cabalistic writing actually tattooed on some part of their body.

Paa-yan

Muay fighters, like all Siamese people, used to have implicit faith in the mystical art of incantation. They studied the subject, believing that incantations would give them miraculous powers to overcome their opponents with ease and endow them with endurance and invincibility, protecting them from all people and things. Some students of the art believed that an incantation uttered before or during a contest had the power to protect them from being knocked out, as a breath of wind would instantly restore them to consciousness. It was also held that such incantations had the ability to counteract the mystical powers which, inevitably, would be invoked by the opponent.

Incantations
(K a r t a r   A r k o m - ค า ถ า อ า ค ม)

The incantation *"Gam Ban Nak Muen"* (literally "Clenched Fist Weighing Ten-thousand [*dhamlueng*]") supposedly gave the fighter the certainty of victory with a single punch. Generally speaking, fighters in the past had tattoos on the back of their hands which incorporated the power of the *"Gam Ban Nak Muen"* incantation. (*Dhamlueng* was a traditional Thai weight; 10,000 *dhamlueng* = 1,000 kilograms.)

These types of incantation were not only part of a rich oral tradition but were in due course printed for reference. Antiquarian books which include such incantations are sometimes still to be found on market stalls and in second-hand book shops in Thailand.

The Tradition of Wai Khru

The following pages present an in-depth study of the unique tradition of *Wai Khru* (Paying Respect to Teachers). Three forms of the ceremony -- Initiation as a Trainee Fighter, Annual Homage-Paying Ceremony and Initiation as a Teacher -- are detailed here, while the fourth form -- Ritual Dance of Homage -- can be found in next chapter as it is very much part of the pre-contest rituals.

For anyone wishing to really understand the central concepts of Muay Thai, a knowledge of at least some of this martial art's unique and rich traditions is an absolute necessity. In fact, for those who are intent on becoming professional fighters or trainers, more than knowledge alone, the precepts and ethics involved have to be come an integral part of their daily lives. Although these traditions are undoubtedly "devout" and imbued with a spirit of religiosity, they are nevertheless independent of any specific creed and therefore are very much accessible to all.

The Concept of
Wai
Khru

(W a i   K h r u - ไหว้ครู)

One of the most important traditions of Muay Thai is *Wai Khru* (Paying Respect to Teachers) and the philosophy which it encapsulates. *Wai Khru* is an ancient custom which is closely bound to the fundamental Thai concept that providers of knowledge are all *khru* -- teachers -- and are worthy of the utmost respect. In the pecking order, parents are everybody's original teachers, while the reigning monarch is the *khru yai* or headmaster. Between teachers -- parents, educators, trainers or mentors -- and their students a special relationship is believed to exist, one which will endure and leave a lasting impression. Likewise, the bond between those who study under the same teacher is regarded as being parallel to kinship, so that such students refer to each other as *pee nong*, brothers and sisters. When students seek knowledge from their teacher, they first offer symbols of respect: flowers, garlands, incense-sticks and candles. If these seem overly religious and more suited to temple offerings, then bear in mind that monks are also teachers while in their own turn being disciples of Buddha: just two more manifestations of the core teacher-student bond.

In order to become a fully-fledged Muay Thai fighter, a person has to pass through a series of ceremonies or "rites of passage" which all come under the generic heading of *Wai Khru*.

First comes the Initiation as a Trainee Fighter Ceremony, in which the *khru muay* (Muay Thai teacher) not only accepts young fighters as his student's, but in return pledges to teach them to the best of his ability. After fighters have been accepted by a teacher, they must demonstrate good conduct, diligence, endurance and other comparable virtues, in addition to training as hard as they can and following implicitly all the teacher's rules.

During their long apprenticeship, young fighters will experience many times the second type of *Wai Khru* ritual, the Annual Homage-Paying Ceremony. This is an annual ceremony, held so that young fighters can pay respect to their teachers -- and to the souls of teachers who have long since passed away -- and culminates in a performance of the Ritual Dance of Homage, the third form of *Wai Khru*.

After training has been underway for some time, they will be sent to take part in a contest, preceded by a performance of the Ritual Dance of Homage as a public declaration of their allegiance to their teacher. It is only when fighters have passed all these three milestones (i.e. initiation, training and participation in contests) that they are entitled to regard themselves as real Muay Thai fighters.

Whether or not fighters can advance to the rank of teacher themselves is a decision which lies in the hands of their own teacher...and the process can take a considerable time. The fighters must first have taken part in numerous contests, proved themselves to have advanced practical skills and have done the equivalent of "teacher training" in both Muay Thai theory and practice, as well as having the right attitude and character. In addition, age plays a part because in Oriental cultures, age and wisdom advance hand in hand. Generally speaking, thirty and over is considered a suitable age for being elevated to the position of *khru muay*.

It is only when fighters have satisfied their teacher on all these counts that they can participate in the fourth *Wai Khru* ritual, the Initiation as a Teacher Ceremony, which bestows on them the rank of *khru muay* and which once again involves a performance of the Ritaul Dance of Homage.

For all forms of the *Wai Khru* rituals except the Ritaul Dance of Homage, fighters have a choice of position while they are paying homage. They can:

      a. kneel sitting back on their heels
      b. half-sit half-kneel in the "mermaid pose"

The important factor is that the fighters' heads must be lower than that of their teacher, symbolizing their lower status and respect.

Why Wai?

(Wai - ไหว้)

The reader who is unfamiliar with Thai culture may well be thinking "What is *wai*?" and "Why *wai*?" What follows is, therefore, a brief "beginner's guide" to this gracious custom and its usage in everyday life, as a basic understanding of the *wai* and its functions in Thai society will enhance the Muay Thai devotee's understanding of the ritualized and traditional elements of this martial art.

Like so many aspects of Thai culture, the origins of the *wai* can be traced back to India. In essence, the *wai* is extremely simple: it involves raising and putting together the palms of the hands and extended fingers. It is a gesture which, accompanied by a verbal salutation or not, conveys a range of sentiments, from a simple "hello" or "goodbye" to a request, expression of gratitude, sign of respect, or an apology.

The subtleties of the gesture can be hinted at in answer to another question: "Who *wai*s who, when and how?" Essentially the position of the hands and head imply degrees of respect and the relative ranks of the individuals involved. Generally speaking, the higher the hands and the greater the degree to which the body and head are inclined, the more respect or obligation is being tacitly expressed in the *wai*. The ultimate *wai* is that offered to the Lord Buddha in any of the country's glittering temples. After adopting the "mermaid" pose with the holy symbols of candle, incense-sticks and lotus flower pressed between their hands, the person paying homage to Buddha will proceed to total prostration (*grarb*), leaning the trunk, arms and face forwards down to the floor. The hands are then slid out to the side and brought together again three times, in an action known as *bae mue*. It is no coincidence that Muay Thai fighters also *bae mue* three times and that the candle, incense-sticks and lotus are also the symbols of respect which they offer to their teacher.

Another important factor in the *wai* is which person initiates the *wai* and which person receives and responds to the *wai*. This depends almost totally on seniority and rank. Generally, the younger must *wai* the elder, the subordinate must *wai* the senior. Two virtual equals in terms of age and rank will rush to *wai*, neither of them wishing to appear to be pulling rank or asserting their superiority by letting the other *wai* first.

There are occasions on which it is optional or entirely inappropriate to return a *wai*, a smile or spoken comment being sufficient. An adult will not return the *wai* of child and persons of high rank or professional/social status may choose not to return the *wai*s of their subordinates. The *wai*s proffered by those in service industries are never returned in kind, a smile or word of thanks for their attention being sufficient.

Sometimes neither party will *wai*. Casual acquaintances, close friends, adult relatives of a similar age who meet frequently and people who have not yet been introduced to each other will not *wai*.

All this forms part of the inherent traditional and religious ramifications when Muay Thai fighters raise their hands in the *wai* to respect their teacher or during the pre-fight rituals. It is clear proof that Muay Thai is an art as much as it is a fighting form, carrying a rich cultural legacy from its roots in Thailand as it becomes increasingly popular in the international arena.

Informing the Spirits Ceremony

(B u w o n g   S u w o n g - บวงสรวง)

The enduring belief of the Thai people in the unseen, the spirits which inhabit all places and which have to be kept happy or, if necessary, appeased when they are angry, is mentioned several times elsewhere in this book. There are visible signs of this redolent animism which coexists quite happily with the dominant Buddhism in the little spirit-houses which are to be found in the corners of many gardens and elsewhere. Looking like little pagodas elevated on a "bird-table", tiny offerings of food and drink will be presented to the occupants, who likewise are informed of any major happenings in the lives of the people in the "big house".

A much more sumptuous and elaborate version of this tradition is the *Buwong Suwong* ceremony which must be held prior to the Annual Homage-Paying Ceremony and Initiation as a Teacher rituals. (In the case of the Initiation as a Trainee Fighter rites, which can be regarded as a personal contract between teacher and newly-accepted student, not involving the spirits of teachers-past, it is an optional requirement.) The ceremony is performed by Brahmin priests who inform the spirits of what is about to take place, ask their permission to proceed and also invite them to attend if they are so inclined.

A special banquet is laid on for the spirits, the menu varying according to a whole range of factors, including the favorite dishes of the particular deity to whom a special appeal is being made. A pig's head, chicken, desserts and fruit are typical offerings, along with candles, incense sticks, flowers and other gifts. The important factor is that, once it has been determined which form of *Buwong Suwong* the ceremony is to take, there is no room for personal choice in the offerings provided: an exact list has to be followed with no omissions or deviations.

After waiting a suitably respectful time -- perhaps about an hour -- to enable the spirits to eat their fill, the human participants in the rites can partake of the feast, which, having been tasted by the spirits, is now full of lucky portents.

Now that the spirits have been made aware of what is to happen and their favor has been sought through the edible offerings, the main ceremony can proceed as planned. The precise details of all the ceremonies differ according to the traditions of the Muay Thai training camp/teacher involved. Invariably, however, all the ceremonies are very powerful and moving, making, as intended, a permanent impression on the participants' minds and helping to stiffen their resolve.

Initiation as a
Trainee
Fighter

(K u e n   K h r u , Yo k   K h r u - ขึ้นครู , ยกครู)

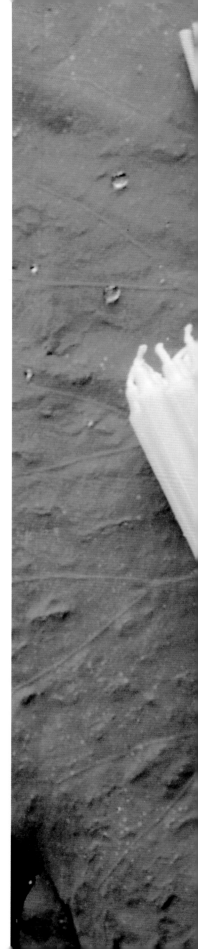

In the past, before a teacher accepted a new student, he first spent a great deal of time considering the proposition, trying to ascertain whether or not the person was really worthy of becoming his student. Some young fighters even initially had to act as servants to their prospective teachers until such time as the teachers were convinced of their suitability and good character. This process sometimes took a year -- or even several years -- to reach a resolution.

When a teacher agrees to accept a new student, the initiation ceremony is held, usually on a Thursday, which is traditionally regarded as *Wan Khru* (Teachers' Day). As they make a formal request to be accepted, the students present the customary symbols of respect to their prospective teacher (*krueng sakkara buchaa khru*). Unlike the set requirements for *Buwong Suwong*, there is some leeway for personal choice, although candles, incense sticks and flowers are invariably included. Another custom-ary offering is a symbolic amount of money, like nine *baht*, "nine" in Thai being *"gao,"* a word which, with a different Thai spelling but identical pronunciation, also means "to step forwards or advance," giving it a hidden propitious significance.

Students pledge in front of the teacher that they will be diligent and hard-working, and that they will respect and obey the teacher, following his rulings to the letter. The teacher, for his part, officially accepts the students and promises to instruct them to the utmost of his abilities.

Annual
Homage-Paying
Ceremony

(W a i   K h r u   P r a j a m   P e e - ไหว้ครูประจำปี)

This ceremony is held annually throughout Thailand in schools, universities or wherever else learning, of whatever sort, takes place. Where Muay Thai is concerned, it is held either on Muay Thai Day (17th March) or any other traditionally propitious day, and requires the trainee fighters to show their respect for and gratitude to their teachers.

Teachers and students alike gather together to arrange the Annual Homage-Paying Ceremony, inviting as many past teachers as possible to attend. The ceremony involves many traditional Thai emblems of honor and respect and commences with all those assembled paying respect to the souls of teachers who have passed away. The ceremony then progresses to the students honoring all the teachers present, who mark sacred symbols on the fighters' foreheads with powder in order to bestow prosperity and success upon them -- a custom know as *jerm*. The ceremony involves the performance of the Ritual Dance of Homage by the fighters as a mark of respect to their teachers, while both teachers and students make sacred vows.

Initiation as a Teacher

(K r o b   K h r u - ครอบครู)

In the *Krob Khru* ceremony, Muay Thai students who have all the necessary qualifications are elevated to the rank of teachers themselves. The teacher has first to consider which students are sufficiently knowledgeable and technically skillful to be worthy of promotion to the ranks of instructor. After the selection has been made, the *Krob Khru* ceremony is held to publicly announce and promote the chosen students who then become teachers in their own right, entitled to pass on the skills and traditions of Muay Thai to students of their own. As in *Kuen Khru,* the teachers-elect offer the traditional symbols of respect to their teacher, who then makes the official proclamation:

> *Today is a propitious day, and this hour of good omen. You have proved yourself to be a person of virtue and knowledge, skilled in the art of Muay Thai, to the extent that you are now worthy of becoming a teacher yourself. I therefore appoint you a newly-created Muay Thai teacher at this Krob Khru ceremony, capable of instructing others in this noble art. Always remember your duty to preserve the traditions and art of Muay Thai. Be a person of good conduct and apply your knowledge and abilities in such a way as to benefit both yourself and the community.*

Musical
Accompaniment to
Muay Thai

In Muay Thai, rhythmic music accompanies the *Wai Khru Ram Muay* rituals as well as the actual contests themselves. This music is referred to as *wong pee glong* and is performed by four musicians, each with their own instrument: *pee chawaa* (Javanese oboe), *glong kaek* (a pair of Thai drums played by two musicians) and *ching* (small Thai cymbals).

Ching With its onomatopoeic name, the *ching* is a percussion instrument which can best be described as a pair of diminutive but comparatively thick cymbals, measuring about 6 - 7 cm. (!less than 3 inches) in diameter, fashioned from bronze or some other metal. The two parts are joined together by a cord which passes through a small hole in the top of each. Unlike Western cymbals which are brought together horizontally and usually fully, the rims only of the *ching* are impacted vertically, the right hand usually being the upper one.

Pee Chawaa This instrument is thought to have originated in India and come into Thailand through Indonesia, hence its name (*chawaa* = Java). The instrument is made from hardwood or ivory or a combination of the two, and consists of two main sections: a cylindrical body about 27cm. (nearly 11 inches) long with seven holes for fingering; and a lower bulbous, bell-shaped section which is about 14 cm. (5 inches) in length. The mouth-piece consists of 2 pairs of reeds attached to a small metal tube which is inserted into the top end of the body of the instrument, the join being made airtight by wrapping thread around it. A small piece of convex metal or, more traditionally, a fragment of coconut shell, functions as a mouth rest or supporter when the instrument is being played. The tone of the *pee chawaa* is, by turns, melancholy and frenetic, the Western oboe being probably the nearest approximation.

Glong Kaek This kind of drum has a cylindrical hardwood body measuring about 58cm. (23 inches) in length. The two heads at either end, which are made from calf- or goatskin tethered by leather thongs, are of unequal size: the lower-toned larger one is 20cm. (8 inches) in diameter, while the higher-toned smaller one measures 18cm. (7 inches). Both drumheads are played with the palms and fingertips. *Glong kaek* are played in differently pitched pairs by two musicians: the higher pitched drum is referred to as *tua poo* (the male), while the lower toned one is known as *tua mia* (the female). A highly sophisticated and complex rhythm is formed by the inter-play between the two drums.

The tempo of the *wong pee glong* music varies according to what it is accompanying. A composition called *"Salamaa"* accompanies the *Wai Khru Ram Muay*: the tempo is slow and stately to match the mood of the rituals, with a smooth, flowing rhythm. When the actual fight commences, a composition called *"Kaeg Chao Sen"* is played .The general tempo of this piece tempo is quicker and, at moments of tension or excitement during the match, it becomes even more frenetic. Undoubtedly, the music increases the atmosphere of the event, while if fighters are not going on the offensive ferociously enough, the music can urge them to rally and try even harder.

Approaching
the Ring
Rites

(K u e n   S u u   W e i t e e - ขึ้นสู่เวที)

In ancient times, as has already been indicated, Siamese people believed in the power of incantations and protective amulets. They thought that everywhere was ruled or inhabited by unseen spirits, and that places were either cursed or blessed. Because of these beliefs, it was necessary to perform special rites before a fighter entered the ring, asking the spirits' permission to do so, propitiating them, and destroying any evil which may be lurking there. The rituals were also thought to protect the fighter and lead him to victory. Even today, the rites involve a strong element of psychology as the fighters psyche themselves in readiness for the imminent bout.

In the days when bouts were staged on the bare ground, fighters used to pay homage to the goddess of the earth, *Mae* Torrannee, by picking up some soil when they were kneeling down and raising it to their forehead. Even in these days of concrete stadiums, some fighters can still be observed pressing their thumb on the floor and then on their forehead. This, like everything else in this particular ritual, is very much a matter of individual preference these days, with no prescribed rules.

The *Wai Khru Ram Muay* can be divided into three main sections:

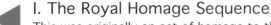

I. The Royal Homage Sequence

This was originally an act of homage to the monarch, going back to the days when the king was a patron of *muay* and fighters were selected to display their skills in front of him. It has three subsections: Prostration, Outstretched Arms and Act of Homage.

II. The Kneeling Sequence

The second section is performed in a kneeling posture, one knee on the ground and the other leg out in the front. You pivot around on the spot to repeat the same sequence facing all four sides of the ring, a tradition which ultimately comes from *krabi krabong*. There is no rigid rule about the order the directions should follow: the important factor is to stick to your teacher's guidelines. If you are practicing by yourself, remember that west -- the direction of the setting sun -- is unlucky in Oriental cultures and so should not be chosen for the first point. These guidelines also apply to "The Standing Sequence".

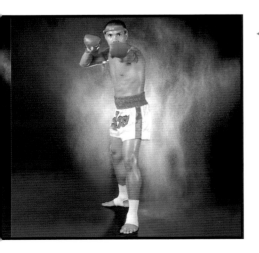

III. The Standing Sequence

In this section, you have to go out from the center of the ring in one direction, perform the Dramatic Interlude, then return and so on until, again, you have been to all four sides. The footwork used is the Ceremonial Form of the Muay Shuffle, (cf. p.127) The Dramatic Interlude demonstrated here is "Rama Shooting an Arrow", an episode from the *Ramakien* in which the hero, Rama, mortally wounds his adversary, Totsagan, with his arrow. The symbolism is obvious!

Removal
of the Head
Circlet

(P i t e e T o d M o n g k o n - พิธีถอดมงคล)

After the *Wai Khru Ram Muay* ritual is completed, the fighters return to
their own corners. Then, they go back to the center of the ring to be
briefed by the referee on the rules of the coming bout and so on. Then,
they return to their own corners once more for the Removal of the Head
Circlet Ritual -- *Pitee Tod Mongkon*.

S t e p b y S t e p

1. Stand in your own corner, facing outwards, while your teacher
   (or an official representative personally appointed by him) stands
   outside the ropes. In a gesture of profound respect, lower your
   head and raise your hands to your chest in the *panom mue wai*
   pose. In response, the teacher then raises his own hands to chest-
   level to return the *wai*.

2. While you maintain the *panom mue wai* posture, the teacher
   utters an incantation and blows three times on the top of your
   head before removing the *mongkon* with both hands.
   Alternatively he caresses the top of your head with one hand
   while holding the *mongkon* in the other, before removing the
   mongkon as before. If you deeply respect your teacher, you
   may then prostrate yourself three times on the floor: this is
   entirely at your own discretion.

On the completion of this ritual, the contest can commence.

CHAPTER 5

Basic Muay Thai Skills

The information provided in this chapter covers the whole range of practical things which you need to do or study before you can even think of starting serious training. Included are some all-purpose warm-up exercises, the method of adopting the Muay Thai stance and some basic first aid in the event of minor cuts and sprains.

Warm-Up
Exercises

You should never begin Muay Thai training -- or that for any other martial art or sport -- without first going through a basic warm-up program which prepares every part of the body for the subsequent action. Any such program should basically target three areas:

1. the cardiovascular system
2. the muscles
3. the joints

Detailed on the following pages are an elementary but effective series of exercises which can be used as a general warm-up, or, indeed, independently.

The Neck

Hold every pose for 3 seconds and repeat the whole set 5 times in all. Please note that it is highly inadvisable to rotate the neck round: it should be brought back to the vertical each time.

Step by Step
1. Hands on hips.
2. Bend neck forwards, chin tucked in.
3. Head up, bend neck over backwards.
4. Neck back to the vertical. Then, head over and down to right shoulder. Head over and down to left shoulder.

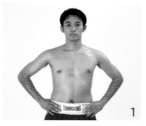

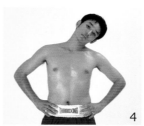

The Shoulders

Rotate 10 times forwards, 10 times backwards, 3 sets.

Step by Step
1. Elbows straight out to the sides, finger tips on shoulders.
2. Elbows forward...
3. ...down...
4. ...and out to the side.

The Waist

The side-to-side swing should be done without pausing at all. Repeat the sequence 10 times, 3 sets.

Step by Step

1. Bend arms, palms inwards, elbows by waist.
2. Twist waist to the left...
3. ...then to the right.

The Chest

Repeat the sequence 10 times, 3 sets.

Step by Step

1. Loosely clenched fists at center of chest, elbows out to the sides.
2. Pull elbows backwards, moving fists outwards. Return to Step 1 pose.
3. Stretch arms diagonally in the rear.

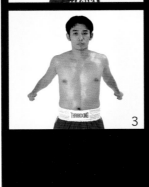

The Ankles

Rotate clockwise and counter-clockwise, 10 times each ankle, each way, 3 sets.

Step by Step

Hands loosely on hips. Raise heel. Pivot round on the ball.

The Knees

Strangely enough, the knee is actually a very weak joint, so as with the neck, under no circumstances should the knees be rotated round and round. Repeat 10 times, 3 sets

Step by Step

1. Bend knees, arch body over, palms on upper part of knees, elbows out to the sides.
2. Straighten knees.

The Hamstrings

a. Do 3 times, holding the pose for 3 seconds, 3 sets. Don't strain if you find it difficult at first to place your palms on the floor.

Step by Step

1. Feet well apart, arms hanging by sides.
2. Bend over, palms on the floor.

a1   a2

b1   b2

c1

c2

b. Do the exercise alternately with your left and right legs, 10 times, 3 sets.

Step by Step

1. Feet in Muay Thai stance, hands loosely in front of thighs.
2. Lean over, right hand on top of right knee, left hand across center left thigh. Pull backwards so right foot goes onto heel, knee fully stretched.

c. Do 3 times with each leg, holding the pose for 10 seconds, 3 sets.

Step by Step

1. Sit on floor, left leg out to side, foot upwards, left hand on lower knee, right hand across upper thigh. Right leg bent, heel tucked into groin.
2. Slide left hand down to ankle, right hand down to knee. Bend over left leg, chest near the thigh, face on knee.

The Inner Thigh Muscle (The Gracilis)

a1

b1

a2

b2

a. Do 3 times with each leg, holding the pose for 10 seconds. Unlike c1 and c2 on the opposite page, it is impossible to bend the body right over this time.

Step by Step
1. Sit on floor. Extend left leg, turned inwards, out to the side. Bend right leg, heel tucked into groin. Raise fists, loosely clenched.
2. Bend trunk as far over to left as comfortable.

b. Do 3 times with each leg, holding the position for 10 seconds, 3 sets. Keep your trunk vertical in Step 2: do not lean forwards.

Step by Step
1. Stand with feet well apart, left foot forwards, right foot out to side. Rest both hands loosely on front of left thigh.
2. Keep trunk vertical. Slide hands down to knee. Bend left knee. Stretch right leg out in the rear.

The Front Thigh Muscle (The Quadriceps)

Do 3 times with each leg and hold the position for 10 seconds, 3 sets.

Step by Step
1. Stand with feet a little apart, arms hanging loosely.
2. Keeping the thigh vertical, bend right knee, raise lower leg backwards and upwards. Use both hands to pull foot to right buttock.

1

2

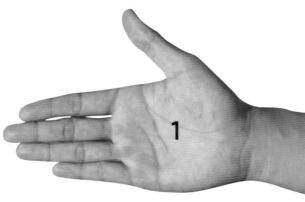

Clenching the Fist

The technique of clenching the fist is an elementary yet important skill: if the fists are clenched correctly, the effectiveness of the punch is increased.

Step by Step

1. Fully extend your four fingers (index, middle, ring and little fingers), holding them close together in a natural manner.
2. Bend the knuckles of all four fingers in sequence: upper, middle...
3. ...and lower, bringing your finger tips in towards your palm.
4. At the same time, fold your thumb over and onto the backs of your index and middle fingers, the tip of your thumb possibly reaching over to your ring finger.

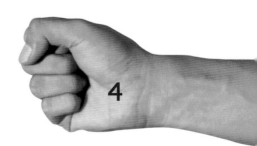

Before you either practice Muay Thai or take part in an actual contest, it is essential that you first apply the hand-wraps to both fists. To fight competitively without these contravenes the regulations. The purpose of wrapping your hands is to protect the back of the fist, the knuckles, the base of the fingers and the wrist from injuries. The gloves must be able to fit snugly over the wrapped fists.

The hand-wraps must not be applied either too tightly or too loosely. When your wrapped hand is clenched into a fist and a punch extended, there should be no sense that the hand-wraps are restricting your movement or are pulling against any part of your hand, or that there is a risk of their becoming loose and slipping.

Hand -Wraps

You can either put on the hand-wraps yourself or get another person to do it for you. If you have a helper, it should be someone who is experienced, and preferably who knows you and the way you train/fight. Don't be afraid to say how you like your hand-wraps to be applied: after all, it is you who are going to be doing the punching!

Although the purpose of the hand-wraps is always the same -- i.e. to protect the fist and wrist from injuries -- there are many differences in the ways in which they can be applied, between training use and contest use.

For the all-purpose method detailed in the following pages, the length of each wrapping strip needs to be about five meters (five and a half yards). The material should be soft, not unduly thick, and definitely not stretchy, because this would constrict your fist, especially when it becomes saturated with either water or sweat.

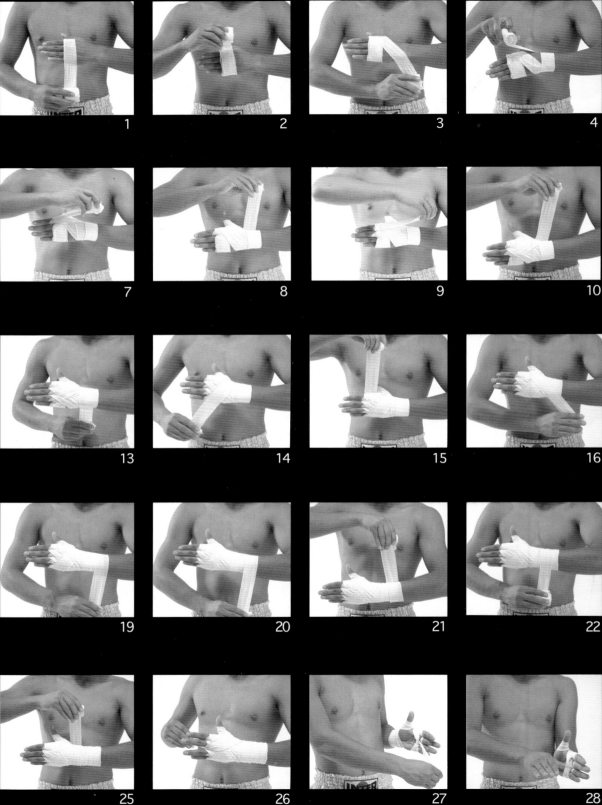

Extend your leg outwards, keeping the knee raised

Raise your lead foot, bending the knee.

Step backwards with your rear foot.

Pull your lead foot back in to your rear foot.

Start

Note: The first step backwards in the Backward Muay Shuffle is invariably taken with the rear foot.

2. Alternating Stance Footwork

Thai: ก้าวเปลี่ยนเหลี่ยม - *Gao Blien Liem*

Focus: A walking action which not only reverses the position of the feet but the whole body alignment.

Variations: Forward (*Rook*), Backward (*Toi*)

Notes: While seeming almost too simple, this method of footwork is invaluable practice in alternating between the right- and left-handed forms of the Muay Thai stance and in being ready to bring weapons on both the right and left sides of the body effectively into action.

Step by Step

Forward Alternating Footwork

1. Step forwards with your right foot.
2. Step forwards with your left foot.
3.

Backward Alternating Footwork

1. Step backwards with your left foot.
2. Step backwards with your right foot.
3.

3. The Step-Slide Shuffle

Thai: สืบเท้า - *Sueb Tao*

Focus: This is a method of footwork in which the feet are either slid along the ground, or are just slightly lifted, and in which the position of the feet is not constantly reversed: they remain in the same position relative to each other.

Variations: Forward (*Rook*), Backward (*Toi*)

Step by Step

Forward Step-Slide Shuffle

1. Move with your left foot, sliding it along the ground or moving it close to the ground
2. Pull your right foot in towards the left, adopting the same technique
3.

Backward Step-Slide Shuffle

1. Move your right foot backwards, as for the forward version
2. Pull your left foot back in towards the right by the same method
3.

4. Diagonal Footwork

Thai: ก้าวฉาก - *Gao Chaak*

Focus: A method of moving diagonally forwards or diagonally backwards, to the left or right, after which the opponent can be attacked from the side.

Variations: Forward (*Rook*) and Backward (*Toi*) to the left and right

Step by Step

Forward Diagonal Footwork to the Left

1. Step forwards with your left foot
2. Pull your right foot sideways, positioning it diagonally behind the left
3.

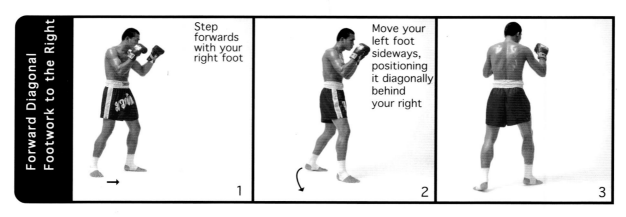

Forward Diagonal Footwork to the Right

1. Step forwards with your right foot
2. Move your left foot sideways, positioning it diagonally behind your right
3.

Backward Diagonal Footwork to the Left

1. Step backwards with your left foot

2. Pull your right foot backwards and over to the left

3.

Backward Diagonal Footwork to the Right

1. Step backwards with your right foot

2. Pull your left foot backwards and over to the right

3.

5. Leg-Block Footwork

Thai: ยกเข่าป้องกัน - *Yok Kow Pong-Gan*

Focus: A method of movement involving raising the knee of each leg alternately, while maintaining a constant readiness to either attack with a foot-thrust or block the opponent's approach with the shin or the knee.

Variations: Forward (*Rook*), Backward (*Toi*)

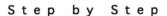

S t e p   b y   S t e p

Forward Leg-Block Footwork			
	Raise your right knee, pointing it forwards and slightly over to your right	Put your right foot down in the front	To contin… raise your left knee, pointing it forwards, slightly ov… to your own left.
	1	2	

Backward Leg-Block Footwork			
	Raise your left knee, pointing it forwards and slightly over to your left.	Put your left foot down in the rear	Then, raise… your right knee point… it forwards and slightly over to your right.
	1	2	

Notes: When adopting the Forward Leg-Block Footwork technique, the first step is always taken with the rear foot, whereas for Backward Leg-Block Footwork, the initial step is taken with the lead foot. This is precisely opposite to the method employed in The Muay Shuffle.

Put your left foot down in the front

4

5

Put your right foot down in the rear

4

5

6. The Boxing Skip

Thai: เต้น - *Dhen*

Focus: Remaining in the Muay Thai stance throughout, with a slight skipping motion the body-weight is constantly shifted between the balls of the two feet in a 90% : 10% ratio.

Notes: As the name suggests, this form of footwork is not part of the Muay Thai tradition but has been incorporated into it from Western boxing.

Step by Step
1. Skipping slightly while maintaining the Muay Thai stance, shift body-weight to front foot.
2. Shift body-weight back to rear foot.

Hint: If you want to progress to using a kick, you must use the leg which is not supporting most of your body-weight!

7. Leaping

Thai: กระโดด - *Gra-dode*

Focus: A method of moving forwards or backwards as fast as possible by utilizing a leap.

Variations: Forward (*Rook*), Backward (*Toi*)

Notes: The thrust from the bent knees and both feet should be used to spring into the air and, when landing, the feet should be in the same respective positions as at take-off.

Step by Step

Leaping Forwards

1. Bending your knees, thrust yourself upwards and forwards, using the force of both feet

2. Land with the feet in the same position as at take-off

3.

Leaping Backwards

1. Bending your kneees, thrust yourself upwards and backwards, using the force of both feet

2. Land with your feet in the same position as at take-off

3.

CHAPTER 7

Muay Thai
Weapons

In its original form, *muay* consisted of an arsenal of nine weapons -- the head, fists, elbows, knees and feet -- known collectively as *na-wa arwud*. Although in modern Muay Thai, both amateur and professional, using the head to butt an opponent is no longer permissible, you still have at your disposal within your own body a formidable fighting force capable of devastating an opponent. Whereas other martial arts which use no other weaponry, like judo, karate and taekwondo, make extensive use of the hands and feet -- and karate and taekwondo both permit the use of elbows and knees in training -- Muay Thai is unique in the way it uses all parts of the body, including the elbows and knees, for both training and competitions. Almost 40 Muay Thai techniques, covering all five attacking methods -- punch, elbow-strike, knee-kick, kick and foot-thrust -- are presented in this chapter.

One of the basic key skills of Muay Thai is learning how to coordinate the four weapons and the five attacking techniques they represent:

Part of the body		Attacking techique	
English	Thai	English	Thai
Fist	*Mud*	Punch	*Shok*
Elbow	*Sork*	Elbow Strike	*Dhee Sork, Fun Sork*
Knee	*Kow*	Knee Kick	*Dhee Kow, Taeng Kow*
Foot	*Tao*	Kick	*Dhe*
		Foot-Thrust	*Teeb*

As the chart shows, there is a one-to-one correlation between weapons and techniques, except in the case of the feet, which can deploy two techniques. *Khru Muay* sometimes ask their students -- especially young fighters -- to remember the following rule:

> Kick loses to punch, punch loses to knee,
> knee loses to elbow, elbow loses to kick

Here kick includes the associated foot-thrust technique. It is a never-ending circle, encapsulating the concept that you must practice and aim to be equally skillful in using all the Muay Thai weapons. To be very good at one but weak in another will put you at an immediate disadvantage!

For the beginner, trying to master even just a few varieties of each technique can very soon add up to a confusing mass of facts and instructions: Should my knee be moving horizontally or diagonally? What should my arms be doing at the same time? Isn't there something else I should be doing? To try to clear the way through at least some of this confusion, the at-a-glance, self-help charts in the Appendix have been formulated. Use them as a quick reference then follow them up with the full details given in this chapter as and when required.

The first photograph in each sequence (marked "Stance") shows the fighter in the Muay Thai Stance, from which all techniques commence. No caption is provided except in the case(s) where an additional comment is necessary.

Punch (Shok - ชก)

Using your clenched fist (*mud*) to punch (*shok*) opponents is an appropriate technique when they are relatively close. The fist is a much easier weapon to control than the foot and one which is also quicker to put into operation. Forming the fist correctly, as detailed in Chapter 5, and using the combined forces of the shoulder, hip and foot to put additional force behind the punch, are both basic yet essential elements in enhancing the power of a punch. In Muay Thai, only the prominent lowest knuckles are used to impact a punch: this is the toughest part of your fist, capable of impacting with the greatest force. (This is different from karate and taekwondo which also use the central knuckles in what is known as the Bear Fist [*Mud Mee*] technique.) Therefore, the word "knuckles" in this section invariably refers to this lowest knuckle ridge.

While you are in the Muay Thai stance, do not clench your fists too stiffly or tightly, but when you are actually using your fist to punch the opponent, the fist should be tightly clenched.

Ideally, you should use both fists to launch an effective attack against the opponent. The fist which is to the fore in the Muay Thai stance is known as *mud nam* or *mud naa* (the lead fist), while the fist on the other side of your body which is in the rear in the Muay Thai stance is known as *mud dhaam* or *mud lang* (the rear fist) -- cf.pp.118-9. It is the rear fist which has the greater power of the two, being on the more dexterous side of your body.

There are many styles of punching in Muay Thai: those listed below are explained in detail in the following pages.

English	Thai	Transliteration
1. Straight Punch	หมัดตรง	*Mud Dhrong*
2. Hook	หมัดเหวี่ยงสั้น	*Mud Wiyang San*
3. Swing	หมัดเหวี่ยงยาว	*Mud Wiyang Yao*
4. Spinning Back Fist	หมัดเหวี่ยงกลับ	*Mud Wiyang Glab*
5. Uppercut	หมัดเสย	*Mud Seuy*
6. Jump Punch	กระโดดชก	*Gra-dode Shok*
7. Overhead Punch	หมัดโขก	*Mud Khouk*

1.The Elbow Slash

Thai: ศอกตี หรือ ศอกฟัน - *Sork Dhee* or *Sork Fun*

Targets: Head, forehead, bridge of the nose, brow bone, eye, temple.

Focus: A method of attacking the opponent by bringing the elbow diagonally downwards against the target, generally at an angle of 45°, almost as if using a sword or a knife to slash the opponent's body.

Step by Step

Stance

1

Stance

1

Notes: This is the most commonly deployed elbow technique.

Tip: Bend your elbow tightly at shoulder level then swing it with full force parallel to the ground

Rear Horizontal Elbow

1. Shift your body-weight onto your left foot, lifting the heel of your right foot off the ground. Simultaneously, raise your tightly bent right elbow to shoulder-level in readiness, the fist by your chin.

2. Boosting its power by twisting your right shoulder and hips and leaning your body forwards, using your right foot as a pivot, forcefully swing your elbow from right to left, parallel to the ground, to impact against the target.

Lead Horizontal Elbow

You can easily adapt this technique for the left elbow by looking at the photos. Your body-weight is still centered on your left foot, but everything else is reversed. Remember! Swing your elbow parallel to the ground!

3. The Uppercut Elbow

Thai: ศอกงัด หรือ ศอกเสย - *Sork Ngad* or *Sork Seuy*

Targets: Chin, jaw, face

Focus: The elbow is thrust diagonally upwards against the target.

Step by Step

Hint: You can bend then extend your knees for additional force if you want. It's up to you!

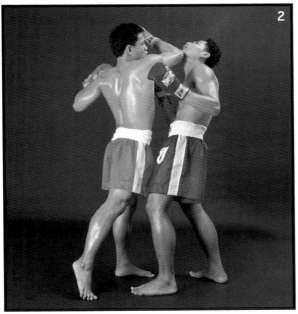

 Rear Uppercut Elbow

1. Center your body-weight on your left leg. Twist your right shoulder, hip and leg somewhat over to the left, pivoting on the ball of your right foot. Bending both your knees as and if required, hold your right elbow in readiness for the attack, the upper-arm horizontal, pointing forwards, the forearm at a slight diagonal so that your fist is by the left side of your face.

2. Thrust your right elbow diagonally up and round, rapidly and forcefully, your fist simultaneously sliding past your left jaw. Impact the point of your elbow against the target.

 Lead Uppercut Elbow

If you want to use your left elbow instead, it is easily done! Your body-weight stays on your left leg as before and your left arm is raised, the fist by the right side of your face. Then thrust the elbow diagonally upwards.

4. The Forward Elbow Thrust

Thai: ศอกพุ่ง - *Sork Poong*

Targets: Head, eyes, brow bone, bridge of the nose, chin

Focus: The attacking elbow is raised then "stabbed" forwards into the target.

Step by Step

Notes: It should be noted that the difference between The Forward Elbow Thrust and The Uppercut Elbow (detailed on the previous pages) lies in the direction in which the elbow is thrust, forwards and sideways respectively. The Forward Elbow-Thrust is usually only deployed by the lead elbow, when the relative positions of the elbow and the opponent make it an appropriate and quite easy technique to utilize.

Hint: If you take a step forwards first with your rear foot so that your right side of your body is now in the front (i.e. you have changed your stance), you can also use your right elbow for this technique.

Lead Forward Elbow Thrust

1. Shift your body-weight to your left leg. Hold your body erect while simultaneously raising your left elbow in readiness to attack, the arm bent with the elbow pointing forwards, the upper-arm horizontal with the ground, the forearm folded back so that the fist is near the left cheek.

2. Thrust the point of your elbow rapidly and powerfully forwards into the target, boosting the power behind your elbow by leaning your body slightly forwards, bending your left knee and full extending your right leg.

5. The Reverse Horizontal Elbow

Thai: ศอกกระทุ้ง หรือ ศอกเหวี่ยงกลับ - *Sork Gratung* or *Sork Wiyang Glab*

Targets: Side of the face

Focus: The elbow is moved horizontally in reverse (i.e. outwards) to impact against the target.

Step by Step

Notes: The Lead Reverse Horizontal Elbow is usually used as a direct offensive move, whereas The Rear Reverse Horizontal Elbow is normally employed as a follow-on move when a planned attack with either The Elbow Slash or The Horizontal Elbow has failed to reach its target, forcefully retracting the elbow along the same trajectory and impacting it against the target.

Tip:
Synchronize the movements of your elbow, shoulder, hip and foot for perfect results.

Rear Reverse Horizontal Elbow

1. Extending your right leg with the foot raised onto the ball, twist your right shoulder and hip round to the left. Bend your right elbow so that both your upper-arm and forearm are parallel to the ground, the fist in front of your chin, in preparation to attack your opponent with The Elbow Slash or The Horizontal Elbow. However, your planned offensive fails to hit the target so you quickly follow on with the reverse action.

2. Swing your right elbow to the right, back along the same path, to hit the target.

Lead Reverse Horizontal Elbow

The Lead Reverse Horizontal Elbow is used as a direct attack because it is much closer to the target already. Simply twist your left shoulder, hip and leg round to the right, while simultaneously bending your left elbow in the same manner. Then swing your left elbow in reverse against the target.

6. The Spinning Elbow

Thai: ศอกกลับ - *Sork Glab*

Targets: Chin, jaw, temple, brow bone, face

Focus: The elbow is used offensively in combination with turning the body round, so that the elbow is extended from the rear

Step by Step

Stance

1

Hint: Remember the rule for the direction of the turn: right elbow, clockwise; left elbow, counter-clockwise.

Reminder: Be aware of what your opponent is up to by looking over your shoulder and keep them view all the time.

Notes: The Rear Spinning Elbow is the basic form of this technique. The Lead Spinning Elbow necessitates first stepping forwards (*gao tao*) and, being therefore slightly more advanced, is included in the "Basic Plus" chapter (q.v.).

Rear Spinning Elbow

1. Pivot in a clockwise half-turn on your left leg, bringing your right leg backwards and round as you do so. At the same time, tightly bend your right elbow so that your fist is near your shoulder, and extend it out to the side, both the upper-arm and forearm parallel to the ground. Turn your head to observe your opponent over your right shoulder.

2. Following on from the momentum of the turn, twisting from the waist and shoulders, and leaning slightly backwards, swing your right elbow, maintained in the same basic position as in Step 1, round to impact against the target.

7. The Elbow Chop

Thai: ศอกสับ - *Sork Sap*

Targets: Face, head, collar-bone

Focus: The elbow is brought down vertically against the target.

Variations: The Double Elbow Chop (*Sork Sap Koo*) (q.v.), in which both elbows are used simultaneously, is a development of this technique

Step by Step

Stance

1

Stance

1

Notes: There are two ways of preparing the elbow to deploy The Elbow Chop technique:

1. raise the arm straight up, then bend the elbow as it is brought downwards against the target.
2. raise and bend the elbow, so that the fist is over the back of the shoulder, and then bring the elbow down.

The former is the more powerful of the two and is the method demonstrated in the photographs.

Remember: The Elbow Chop and the Double Elbow Chop can only be used effectively against an opponent of lower stature or if the opponent is stooping.

 ### Rear Elbow Chop

1. Raise your body by going up onto the toes of one or both feet, depending on the relative positions of the opponent/target, and twist your right shoulder, hip and fully-extended leg over to the left. Simultaneously, raise your right elbow in readiness to attack, the upper-arm close to the side of your head, your elbow bent, your right fist above your head.

2. Putting your body-weight behind your right elbow, chop it downwards forcefully and rapidly, with the palm of your hand facing in towards your face, to impact against the target.

 ### Lead Elbow Chop

If you are using the left elbow, there is no need to twist your body round, just "raise and chop". All the other details are the same!

8. The Double Elbow Chop

Thai: ศอกสับคู่ - Sork Sap Koo

Targets: Face, head, collar-bone

Focus: Both the elbows are raised, then simultaneously brought vertically downwards to impact against the target.

Step by Step

Stance

1

Notes: The Double Elbow Chop is most commonly deployed when the two fighters are grasping each other's necks with both arms. The fighter whose arms are outside can quickly employ this technique as a way of counteracting the opponent's intended attack with the knee. (cf. p.183).

Hint: As an alternative, try raising both arms with your hands above your head, then chopping the elbows down as you've already done for The Elbow Chop.

Double Elbow Chop

1. Raise your body by going up onto the toes of one or both feet, depending on the relative positions of the opponent/target. Simultaneously, raise your elbows in readiness to attack, the upper-arms close to the sides of your head, elbows bent, the fists over your sholders.

2. Putting your body-weight behind your elbows, and twisting somewhat to the left, forcefully and rapidly chop them downwards to impact against the target, the palm of the hands facing in towards your face.

9. The Mid-Air Elbow Strike

Thai: กระโดดศอก - *Gra-dode Sork*

Targets: Head, face, collar-bone

Focus: A technique which utilizes one of the forms of elbow strike while actually in mid-air, with both feet off the ground, or at the point of landing. Landing can be done on both feet or just one, although invariably the feet maintain their basic Muay Thai stance position.

Step by Step

Stance

1

Variations: Any type of elbow strike can be used in combination with the jump, for example The Horizontal Elbow, The Elbow Slash etc. The photographs show The Elbow Chop being used.

Notes: This is a very effective and rapid means of attack because the force of the body-weight is combined with the power of the elbow itself

Tip: To make this technique effective, you should aim to get quite a bit of height into your jump so that your elbow can impact really forcefully against the target.

Jump + Rear Elbow Chop

1. Spring into the air off both feet, bending your knees for extra thrust. Twist your body over to the left, while simultaneously preparing your right elbow as described in The Rear Elbow Chop (q.v.). Hold your left arm naturally rather than in a strictly defensive attitude.

2. At the point of landing, chop your elbow down against the target.

Knee-Kick

(D h e e K o w - ตีเข่า)

The bony joint between your femur (thigh-bone) and tibia (shin-bone), including the patella (knee-cap), which protrudes when the leg is bent, is another offensive weapon in the Muay Thai arsenal.

A knee-kick (*Dhee Kow* or *Taeng Kow* in Thai) involves bending and raising your knee, then striking the target with either the point of your knee or the inner part of the knee-joint. When you deploy your knee in this way, make sure that your toes are extended straight downwards in a continuous line from your shin to increase its sharpness and power.

The basic forms of knee-kick listed below are detailed in the following pages.

English	Thai	Transliteration
1. Straight Knee-Kick	เข่าตรง	*Kow Dhrong*
2. Diagonal Knee-Kick	เข่าเฉียง	*Kow Chiyang*
3. Curving Knee-Kick	เข่าโค้ง	*Kow Kouwng*
4. Horizontal Knee-Kick	เข่าตัด	*Kow Dhad*
5. Knee Slap	เข่าตบ	*Kow Dhob*
6. Knee Bomb	เข่าโยน	*Kow Youwn*
7. Flying Knee-Kick	เข่าลอย	*Kow Loy*
8. Step-Up Knee-Kick	เข่าเหยียบ	*Kow Yiep*

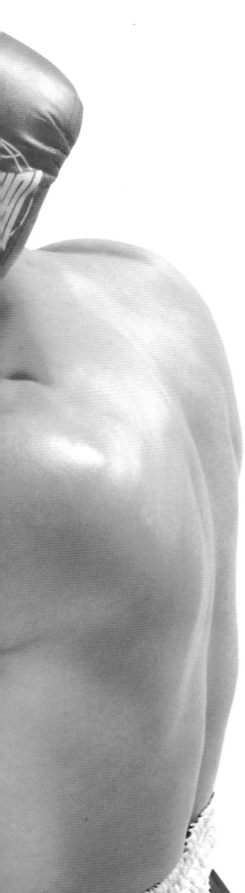

Almost all forms of the knee-kick can originate from the basic Muay Thai Stance. When you are practicing (or have no partner available), use only your knee without grasping the opponent's neck with your hands. This lessens the power of impact but it is a good form of training. However, with one or two exceptions, the different knee-kicking techniques are generally used in combination with one or both hands, which grasp and pull on the opponent's neck in the direction of the on-coming knee as it is being thrust towards the target. The photos therefore illustrate this combined "pull and thrust" technique.

You should always aim to grasp the opponent's neck from the inside (i.e. inside the opponent's arms) as this enables you to secure the firmest grip. If you grasp from the outside (i.e. allowing your opponent's arms to be inside your own) your hold on the neck can be easily knocked away. However, a word of warning: although the "arms inside" rule is undoubtedly best, it does give your opponent the opportunity to launch an elbow attack, so be on your guard!

You can bring the knee-kick into play when the opponent is at close quarters, and occasionally in a long-range attack, like The Flying Knee-Kick. You should incline your head and tuck in your chin when using your knee offensively, but be careful: do not fall into the trap of lowering your eyes as well as your head. Watch your opponent closely, as they will invariably counter with a punch or an elbow strike.

In addition to being an offensive weapon, you can also use your knee defensively, as it offers effective protection against your opponent's knee-kicks or foot-thrusts (cf. Chapter 8, "Basic Plus", p.274-5)

Grasping the opponent's neck with the arms correctly positioned on the inside.

1. The Straight Knee-Kick

Thai: เข่าตรง - *Kow Dhrong*

Targets: Abdomen, solar plexus

Focus: Grasping and pulling the opponent's neck with both hands, the knee is raised directly to impact against the target.

Step by Step

Stance

1

Stance

1

Notes: The Straight Knee-Kick can be conveniently thought of as the knee equivalent of The Straight Kick (*Dhe Dhrong*)

Reminder: Your face should be slightly inclined, with your chin tucked in protectively against the base of the throat. Remember to observe your opponent closely!

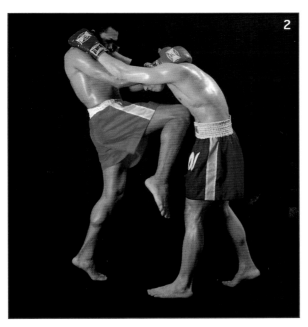

◀ Rear Straight Knee-Kick

1. Lean forwards, transferring your body-weight to your left foot, and firmly grasp your opponent's neck with both hands.

2. With a twist of the right hip over to the left for extra force, thrust your right knee up against the target, the toes of your right foot pointing directly downwards to the floor, while simultaneously pulling down on your opponent's neck. (When adopting this method, your body will naturally lean slightly backwards, with the heel of your left foot raised off the ground).

◀ Lead Straight Knee-Kick

If you wish to employ this technique with your left knee, here are the basics. Body-weight on your right foot, grasp your opponent's neck. Thrust your left knee up (Remember the toes!) while pulling down on your opponent's neck.

2. The Diagonal Knee-Kick

Thai: เข่าเฉียง - *Kow Chiyang*

Targets: Thigh, rib-cage, side of the body

Focus: Grasping and pulling the opponent's neck with both hands, the knee is raised diagonally and impacted against the target.

Step by Step

Reminder:
Remember to grasp your opponent's neck from the inside... and then be on your guard in case you become the victim of an elbow attack!

Rear Diagonal Knee-Kick

1. Lean forwards, transferring your body-weight to your left foot, and firmly grasp your opponent's neck with both hands.

2. Thrust your right knee diagonally upwards at an angle of approximately 45° from right to left, the toes of this foot stretched straight down. Simultaneously, pull diagonally downwards from left to right on the opponent's neck, bracing your left foot against the floor. Impact your knee-cap forcefully against the target.

Lead Diagonal Knee-Kick

Here are the basic elements involved in using your left knee. Lean forwards, body-weight on your right foot, and grasp your opponent's neck. Thrust your left knee diagonally upwards from left to right, while pulling diagonally downwards on your opponent's neck from right to left.

3. The Curving Knee-Kick

Thai: เข่าโค้ง - *Kow Kouwng*

Targets: Thigh, rib-cage

Focus: The knee is initially raised higher than the intended target, then brought round and down in a curving movement to impact against it, with the lower leg bent backwards and upwards, the toes stretched straight.

Step by Step

Rear Curving Knee-Kick

1. Lean forwards, putting your body-weight on your left leg. Extend your right hand, little finger uppermost, towards the opponent and grasp the right side of their neck.

Tip: Don't
forget to extend
your toes in a
straight line,
parallel with your
shin.

2. Lean your body over to your own left and raise your right knee higher than the intended target. Make sure your lower right leg is angled slightly backwards with the toes extending in a straight line.

3. Twist your right hip round and over to the left, using the ball of your left foot as the pivot, as you bring your right knee round and down against the target in a curving movement, simultaneously pulling your opponent's neck downwards with your right hand.

Continued >

The Curving Knee-Kick
Continued

Stance

Lead Curving Knee-Kick

1

To use the left leg, in brief, put your body-weight on your right leg. Leaning forwards, grasp the left side of your opponent's neck with your left hand as before. Using your right foot as the pivot, twist your body from left to right as you raise your left knee then bring it in a curve round and down to impact your knee-cap against the target.

Reminder:
Remember to protect the chin-to-waist line with your other arm. Otherwise, it will be wide open to attack.

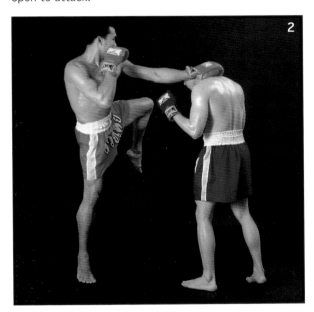

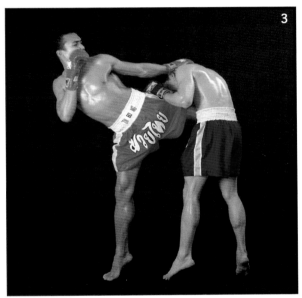

5. The Knee-Slap

Thai: เข่าตบ - *Kow Dhob*

Targets: Trunk, rib-cage

Focus: Grasping and pulling the opponent's neck with both hands, the knee is raised high in the air to the same level as the intended target and the inner part of the knee-joint is used to slap sideways against it.

S t e p   b y   S t e p

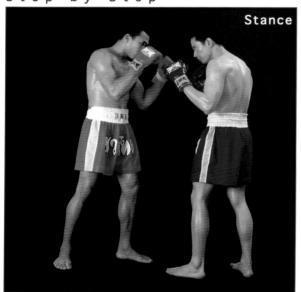

Stance

▲ **Rear Knee-Slap**

1

1. When your opponent is in close proximity, grasp his neck with both your hands.

Tip: You need to go up onto the toes of your supporting leg to get the height and pivotal movement necessary for a successful attack.

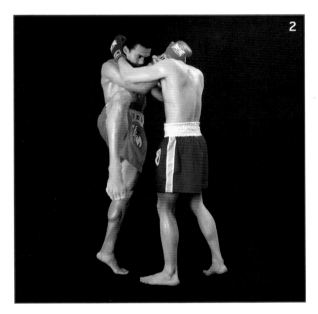

2. With your body-weight on your left leg, raise your right knee out to the side to the same level as the intended target, with the lower leg and toes in a smooth line pointing straight down in the same manner as The Horizontal Knee-Kick.

3. Pivoting on the ball of your left foot, twist your right hip over to the left, and, while using your hands to pull the opponent's neck sideways from left to right, slap the inner part of your knee-joint horizontally from right to left against the target.

Continued >

The Knee-Slap
Continued

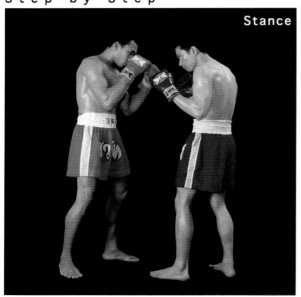

Stance

Lead Knee-Slap

1

You can easily adapt these rules for your left leg. Grasp your opponent's neck with both hands as before, but put your body-weight on your right leg. Raise your left knee out to the side, lower leg straight down, then, pivoting on the ball of your right foot, at the same time pull your opponent's neck over to the left, twist your left hip round to the right, and slap the inner part of your knee against the target.

Tip: Remember to keep your head down but not your eyes!

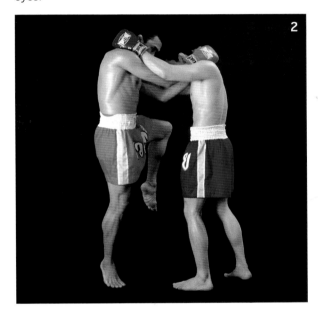

6. The Knee Bomb

Thai: เข่าโยน - *Kow Youwn*

Targets: Abdomen, solar plexus

Focus: The knee is raised and thrust forwards against the target in a sliding or skidding movement. The hands are not used to grasp the opponent's neck.

Step by Step

Stance

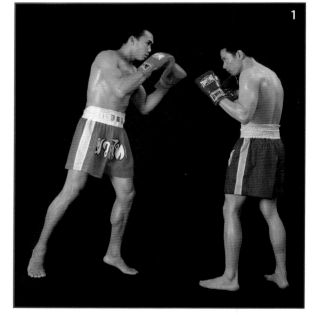
1

Stance

1

Notes: This technique requires great expertise and can be used only when the opponent is bending their knees excessively. The rear leg is almost invariably used to execute this technique.

Tip: Your foot must be placed with the sole going across the thigh in order to get a good grip, not running parallel along it, as this would result in slipping.

Rear Step-Up Knee-Kick

1. When the opponent is in the opposite stance to yourself and with knees bent more than usual, step with your left foot onto the opponent's right thigh. Lift your right heel off the ground in readiness and extend your left arm out in the front, protecting your face with your right fist.

2. Grasping the right side of the opponent's neck with your right hand, little finger uppermost, and pushing with the toes of your right foot, raise yourself up on your left foot, the opponent's thigh functioning as a "step". Then quickly thrust your right knee forwards to impact the knee-cap against the target.

Kick (Dhe – เตะ)

Dhe (kicking) involves swinging some part of your lower leg, from the upper shin down to the foot, to strike against the target. (For the basic differences between Kicks and Foot-Thrusts, cf.p.234.) You can use either your lead foot *(tao naa)* or rear foot *(tao lang)* to kick, although there are some important distinctions:

	Advantages	Disadvantages
Rear Foot	More powerful	Slower
	Can move more freely	Opponent easily anticipates your attack
Lead Foot	Faster	Less powerful
	Less chance of opponent anticipating your attack	Less freedom of movement

Muay Thai has many different kicking techniques, those listed below being detailed in the following pages.

English	Thai	Transliteration
1. Straight Kick	เตะตรง	*Dhe Dhrong*
2. Nutcracker Kick	เตะผ่าหมาก	*Dhe Paa Maak*
3. Round Kick	เตะตัด	*Dhe Dhad*
4. Diagonal Kick	เตะเฉียง	*Dhe Chiyang*
5. Half-Shin, Half-Knee Kick	เตะครึ่งแข้งครึ่งเข่า	*Dhe Krueng Kheng Krueng Kow*
6. Spinning Heel Kick	เตะกลับหลัง	*Dhe Glab Lang*
7. Down Round Kick	เตะกด	*Dhe Kod*
8. Axe Heel Kick	เตะโขก	*Dhe Khouk*
9. Jump Kick	กระโดดเตะ	*Gra-dode Dhe*
10. Step-Up Kick	เหยียบเตะ	*Yiep Dhe*

1. The Straight Kick

Thai: เตะตรง - *Dhe Dhrong*

Targets: Chin and surrounding area

Focus: After raising the leg, knee bent, kick the target with the ball of the foot or the instep. However, when you use the instep, be careful that the toes do not get in the way and so reduce the power of the kick.

Step by Step

Stance

1

Stance

1

Variation: The Nutcracker Kick (q.v.) is a version of The Straight Kick using the instep and targeting a lower level (specifically the groin).

Note: This technique should not be confused with a foot-thrust (*teeb*), although the ball of the foot is used, the movement is an upward "snap", rather than a forward thrust.

Hint: You can keep both fists up protectively as you attack or you may prefer to swing one downwards and backwards for balance, especially if you go up onto the ball of your foot as you atack.

Rear Straight Kick

1. Put your body-weight on your left leg and, leaning very slightly backwards, bend and raise your right knee high up, your right foot pointing towards the target.

2. Twisting your right hip over to the left, swing your right leg, using the power gained from the upwards movement to kick the ball of the foot against the target.

Lead Straight Kick

The instructions are easily adapted to make them applicable to the lead foot: put your body-weight on your right leg this time, lean backwards slightly, bend and raise your left knee, then kick out with the ball of your foot against the target. Remember: you do not have to twist the left hip unduly as it is already in the front.

2. The Nutcracker Kick

Thai: เตะผ่าหมาก - *Dhe Paa Maak*

Targets: Groin

Focus: Involves raising the foot upwards from the ground in a slicing movement, to target the opponent's groin with the shin or instep.

Step by Step

Notes: A technique, used when close to the opponent, which is capable of inflicting great pain. It should be stressed that nowadays this movement is against the rules of both professional and amateur Muay Thai. However, it is a very useful "weapon" in the event of having to respond to a real-life assault.

Rear Nutcracker Kick

1. Put your body-weight on your left leg and, twisting your right hip round to the front, raise your right leg, bent at a 90° angle at the knee, the toes pointing downwards.

2. Straightening your knee and leaning backwards, but keeping your head and neck vertical, slice your right leg vertically upwards between your opponent's legs, impacting your shin or instep against the groin.

Lead Nutcracker Kick

To adapt the instructions to make them applicable to the left foot, first put your body-weight on your right leg and raise your left leg, bent at the knee. Straighten and slice your leg upwards, leaning backwards as you do so.

3. The Round Kick

Thai: เตะตัด - *Dhe Dhad*

Targets: Head and sholders (High Round), trunk (Middle Round), legs (Low Round)

Focus: The leg is swung against the target, while the hips and trunk are simultaneously twisted in the same direction as the swing. The shin or instep is impacted against the target in a slicing or pressing action.

Step by Step

Variations:

 High Round
b. Middle Round
c. Low Round (Inner Knee, Thigh, or Outer Knee)

Notes: This technique is unique to Muay Thai and, of all the kicking methods, it is the one most frequently used.

Tip: Your body should bend naturally over to the side along with the twist of your hip.

Rear High Round

1. Pivot to the left on the ball of your left foot, raise your right leg, bent at the knee, your lower leg extending to the side, and twist your right hip over to the left.

2. Use the accumulated force from Step 1 to continue twisting your right hip and trunk further to the left. Swing your right leg up and out from the knee, extending your right arm for balance. Use your lower shin, or the juncture of your shin and instep, to impact against the target.

Lead High Round

Follow the same basic instructions as for the right foot, not forgetting to lean over to the right as you raise and swing your left leg. You need to get it high up to hit the target effectively!!

Continued >

The Round Kick
Continued

Stance

1

Stance

1

Variations:

a. High Round

b. Middle Round

c. Low Round (Inner Knee, Thigh, or Outer Knee)

Remember:
The Low Round to the Thigh and The Low Round to the Outer Knee are not applicable to the lead foot

Rear Low Round to the Thigh

1. Prepare yourself for the kick in the same way as for The Low Round to the Inner Knee

2. Then, swing your leg outwards and slightly upwards, impacting your lower shin (or shin/instep) against your opponent's thigh.

Rear Low Round to the Outer Knee

1. Again, the preparatory step follows the same pattern as the other Low Round kicks.

2. Then, swing your leg outwards and downwards, leaning your body over backwards more than usual, and impact your instep against the target, the crook of the opponent's knee or the back of the calf.

4. The Diagonal Kick

Thai: เตะเฉียง หรือ เตะริด - *Dhe Chiyang* or *Dhe Rid*

Targets: Rib-cage

Focus: A technique in which the leg is brought diagonally upwards, the foot moving at an angle of 45° to the ground, striking the shin (or occasionally the instep) against the target.

Step by Step

Stance

1

Stance

1

Tip: Swing your arm out naturally with your leg for rhythm and balance.

Rear Diagonal Kick

1. Put your body-weight on your left leg and, twisting your right hip over to the left (but to a lesser extent than for The Round Kick) raise your right leg, bent at the knee, which points over to the left. The lower leg is therefore at an approximate 45° angle, the shin and the toes being in a continuous straight line.

2. Finally, lash your lower right leg diagonally upwards from right to left against the target.

Lead Diagonal Kick

When using your lead foot to execute the move, here are the rules in brief: Body-weight, right leg. Left leg raised, bent at the knee. Lash lower left leg diagonally upwards from left to right. Remember to keep your shin and toes in a straight line and that you do not have to twist your left hip unduly as it is already in the front.

5. The Half-Shin, Half-Knee Kick

Thai: เตะครึ่งแข้งครึ่งเข่า - *Dhe Krueng Khaeng, Krueng Kow*

Targets: Trunk, rib-cage, abdomen

Focus: Maintaining the angle of the bent knee, the upper shin is thrust and pressed against the target.

Step by Step

Stance

1

Stance

1

Notes: This is a technique which is generally used when the opponent is at close quarters. It can be visualized as a combination of a kick and a knee-kick. There are several noticeable similarities between this technique and The Knee Bomb (q.v.).

Tip: You need to make sure that your body is very stable otherwise you'll go off-balance as you keep your leg rammed against the target.

Rear Half Shin, Half-Knee Kick

1. With your body-weight on the ball of your left foot, which becomes the base for the move, raise and bend your right knee at an approximate 110° angle, simultaneously twisting your right hip round to the front, leaning your body a little over to the left in a natural manner.

2. Maintaining your knee bent at the same angle, and bringing your lower leg forward and round, thrust and keep your upper shin pressed against the target.

Lead Half-Shin, Half Knee Kick

Here are the rules in brief for the lead foot. Body-weight on your right foot, raised onto the ball. Left leg raised, bent at the knee, lower leg out to the side. Straighten and swing the left leg up and round. Impact your upper shin against the target. Again, remember that you do not have to twist the left hip unduly as it is already in the front.

6. The Spinning Heel Kick or "The Crocodile Tail Thrash"

Thai: เตะกลับหลัง หรือ จระเข้ฟาดหาง - *Dhe Glab Lang* or *Jerakhae Faad Hang*

Targets: Temple, ear, neck, jaw, chin, head

Focus: The body is rapidly twisted around while simultaneously kicking the leg out in the rear towards the opponent, impacting the heel against the target.

Step by Step

Stance

1

 Rear Spinning Heel Kick

1. Pivoting on both feet, but with your body-weight primarily on the right, twist your hips and trunk quickly clockwise, bringing your head round sharply to look over your right shoulder, so that the opponent is out of your sight for the shortest possible time.

Variations: Theoretically, either leg can be employed to execute The Spinning Heel Kick, depending on the circumstances, and it can be employed either as a follow-on to a failed kick or as an offensive move in its own right. The basic version, using the rear foot as an offensive move, is detailed here When you are confident about using this, you can progress to trying slightly more complex forms, like the one given in the "Basic Plus" chapter, pp.266-7

Notes: Even though this technique involves turning your back, it is essential that you continue to closely observe the opponent.

2. Shift your body-weight to the left foot and, still observing the opponent over your shoulder, begin to swing your right leg out to the rear.

3. Pivoting on your left foot so that it points out to the left and leaning your body over to the left, continue swinging your right leg round and up to impact the heel against the target.

7. The Down Round Kick or "The Coiled Dragon's Tail"

Thai: เตะกด หรือ นาคาขนดหาง - *Dhe Kod,* or *Naakhaa Khanod Haang*

Targets: Neck, collar-bone, side of face

Focus: One foot is raised diagonally upwards, until it is higher than the intended target. From this elevated position, with the leg slightly bent, the lower shin and/or instep is swung round and down to impact against the target.

Step by Step

 Rear Down Round Kick

1. Put your body-weight on your left leg and, bending over to the left, raise your right knee as high as possible.

Notes: An extremely powerful technique which is commonly employed when the opponent is ducking down, or against an opponent of smaller stature. Using your lead foot to execute this kick is also possible but it is more advanced and difficult to use with accuracy and force. If you miss the target using this technique, the opponent will easily be able to come in and attack and put you off balance. So practice carefully before you put it into use.

Hint: Although at the point of impact for this technique and The Spinning Heel Kick are very similar, in preparation they are markedly different. Familarize yourself carefully with them both.

2. Twisting your body round and over to the left, extend your leg and bring it diagonally upwards to its highest intended position.

3. Then swing your leg round and down, impacting your right lower shin and/or instep against the target.

8. The Axe Heel Kick

Thai: เตะโขก - *Dhe Khouk*

Targets: Head, collar-bone

Focus: The extended leg is lifted straight up to its highest position then brought crashing vertically downwards to impact the heel against the target.

Step by Step

Notes: A technique utilized when the opponent is ducking down, or against an opponent of lower stature. Although the ideal target is the head, this is extremely difficult to achieve: the collar-bone is a more realistic -- and easily broken -- point of impact.

Tip: As with all the high-kicking techniques, it is easy to lose your balance. Be aware of this and use your arm and general body posture to keep your equilibrium.

Rear Axe Heel Kick

1. Shift your body-weight to your left leg. Twist your right hip a little and raise your right leg straight up in the air, higher than the intended target.

2. When your leg is in its highest possible position, bring your heel crashing down against the target, twisting your left foot round to the left as feels suitable with the momentum of the action.

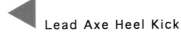

Lead Axe Heel Kick

Once again, it is easy to apply these instructions to the left leg. You can probably work it out for yourself, but here are the main points. Body-weight: right leg, keeping your balance. Left leg: raised straight up, higher than the target. Left heel: crashed down onto the target. Remember: you do not have to twist your left hip this time because it is already in the front.

9. The Jump Kick

Thai: กระโดดเตะ - *Gra-dode Dhe*

Targets: Face, rib-cage, trunk, chin, neck, head

Focus: Involves springing off the ground using the thrust from both feet. One foot, invariably that on the more dexterous side of the body, is then used to kick the target.

Step by Step

 Jump + Rear Round Kick

 1. Bend both your knees in preparation for the jump.

Variations: Although technically any kicking technique can be used in combination with The Jump Kick, in practice The Round Kick is almost always used. Occasionally, The Down Round Kick is coupled with The Jump Kick.

Hint: It is important that you bend your knees to get the required amount of "spring" for the jump

 2. Using both feet to obtain the required leverage, spring into the air, twisting your right hip forwards, and extending your right leg, bent at the knee, out to the side, with the lower leg in the rear. This can be thought of as a mid-air version of the preparation for The Round Kick.

3. Finally, holding your arms in a natural manner to help preserve your balance, straighten your right leg, swinging your right foot up and round against the target

10. The Step-Up Kick

Thai: เหยียบเตะ - *Yiep Dhe*

Targets: Face, chin, jaw, head

Focus: The lead foot is used to step up on the opponent's thigh, while simultaneously the rear foot kicks the target.

Step by Step

 Rear Step-Up Kick

1. Seeing that your opponent is in the opposite stance to yourself with the knee noticeably bent, step up on your opponent's right thigh with your left foot

Notes: A technique which can be brought into play when the knee(s) of the opponent are bent. The lead foot is virtually never used to execute this technique.

Tip: Remember to place your foot crosswise on your opponent's thigh to get a good grip and leverage. Don't put it lengthwise...it will slip very easily!

 2. Then raise your whole body up on this base, using the leverage thus obtained to launch your body upwards and outwards. At the same time, twist your right hip round and over to the left, and bend your right leg at the knee, with the lower leg and foot to the rear. Extend your right arm forwards while holding your left arm, still bent at the elbow, out to the side.

 3. Finally, swing your leg outwards and forwards to impact against the target dramatically while you are in mid-air.

Foot-Thrust
(T e e b - ถีบ)

A foot-thrust (*teeb*) is the method of extending your leg, initially bent at the knee, and thrusting the toes, ball of the foot, sole or heel against the target. It is a technique which you can use either offensively, or as a means of blocking or counteracting the opponent's attack, knocking him/her off balance and then swiftly taking the opportunity to swing out a kick (cf. Chapter 8 "Basic Plus" p.268). You can use either foot to execute this technique, depending on the circumstances, although you will find that the rear foot (*tao dhaam / tao lang*) is more powerful and effective.

Although both kicking and foot-thrusting use basically the same part of the body, you should recognize the distinguishing features of the ways in which the two techniques are deployed. It is also true to say that a foot-thrust is more of a temporizing move than a kick, having three main functions:

    a. to push the opponent away
    b. to destroy the opponent's rhythm
    c. to put the opponent off-balance

In general, a foot-thrust is quickly followed by an attack using another weapon from the Muay Thai arsenal, in the same way as The Jab is deployed as the first part of a two-pronged attack.

Muay Thai has a variety of foot-thrusting techniques, those listed here being detailed in the following pages.

English	Thai	Transliteration
1. Straight Foot-Thrust	ถีบตรง	*Teeb Dhrong*
2. Sideways Foot-Thrust	ถีบข้าง	*Teeb Kang*
3. Reverse Foot-Thrust	ถีบกลับหลัง	*Teeb Glab Lang*
4. Slapping Foot-Thrust	ถีบตบ	*Teeb Dhob*
5. Jumping Foot-Thrust	กระโดดถีบ	*Gra-dode Teeb*

Note: In the photos illustrating all the foot-thrusting techniques, the opponent is in the left-handed stance, enabling the points of impact to be observed more clearly

1. The Straight Foot-Thrust

Thai: ถีบตรง - *Teeb Dhrong*

Targets: Chest, solar plexus, abdomen, groin

Focus: Involves raising the leg, bent at the knee, then thrusting the foot straight out to impact against the target.

Step by Step

Stance

1

2b

2c

Variations: There are 4 basic forms of The Straight Foot-Thrust, using, respectively, the toes *(Teeb Jik)*, ball of the foot *(Teeb Soh)*, sole *(Teeb Yan)* and heel *(Teeb Tink)* to impact against the target.

Notes: Although targeting the groin with this technique is effective in the case of an actual assault, remember that it is "off-limits" in both the professional and amateur Muay Thai ring.

Tip: Practice using all 4 parts of your foot to hit the target. Be aware of which you find the easiest and work on those with which you have a bit more difficulty.

Rear Straight Foot-Thrust

1. Put your body-weight on your left-leg and raise your right leg, the knee bent at a 90° angle, the toes pointing forwards.

2. Twisting your right hip and thrusting your right leg straight out, use
   a. your toes, tightly pressed together
   b. the ball of your foot, fully exposed by straining your toes backwards
   c. the sole of your foot
   d. your heel
   to impact against the target

2d

Continued >

The Straight Foot-Thrust
Continued

Step by Step

Stance

1

2b

2c

Remember:
Keep your fist
raised defensively
and scrutinize
your opponent
throughout

Lead Straight Foot-Thrust

To try this technique with the front foot, raise your left leg, bent at the knee, and then thrust it straight out. As usual, it is not necessary to twist the left hip, as it is already to the fore. The same four variations are possible, using

> a. your toes
> b. the ball of your foot
> c. the sole of your foot
> d. your heel

to impact against the target.

2. The Sideways Foot-Thrust

Thai: ถีบข้าง - *Teeb Kang*

Targets: Abdomen, solar plexus, chest, neck

Focus: Involves thrusting out to the side with the foot while twisting the body sideways-on to the opponent. The outer edge or sole of the foot is used to impact against the target, the latter being easier and more common.

Step by Step

Notes: This is a technique which, although seldom used in Muay Thai, is frequently incorporated into taekwondo and karate. This is because the basic stance for these two martial arts is more acutely sideways-on than in Muay Thai and therefore the technique can be the more easily deployed.

Reminder: Let your arm extend naturally as you thrust your foot forwards: it will add to the power and act as a stabilizer.

Rear Sideways Foot-Thrust

1. Pivot to the left on your left foot, while bringing your right hip round to the front. At the same time, pull your right leg, knee tightly bent, up and into your body, leaning back and over to the left. Your right shoulder, hip and heel are thus in a straight diagonal line pointing to the target.

2. Thrust you right leg forwards so that the sole of the foot impacts against the target.

Continued >

The Sideways Foot-Thrust
Continued

Stance

1

 Lead Sideways Foot-Thrust

As the photos show, using the lead foot involves an optional addition, in which the right foot is brought close up to the left before thrusting out. It all depends on your rhythm, the position of the opponent and so on. Otherwise, the method is the same.

Tip: Make sure you pull your knee well into your body in order to achieve maximum thrust

3. The Reverse Foot-Thrust

Thai: ถีบกลับหลัง - *Teeb Glab Lang*

Targets: Abdomen, solar plexus, chest

Focus: This involves turning backwards-on to the opponent, then raising the leg and extending it straight out to thrust against the target with the heel or sole of the foot.

Step by Step

Stance

1

 Rear Reverse Foot-Thrust

 1. Commence the clockwise half-turn, both your feet and fists remaining in their basic positions. Quickly turn your head to look over your right shoulder to get the target in your field of vision again, while twisting your right foot further round, raising the heel of your left foot.

Hint: Why don't you compare the preparatory movements for this technique with those for The Spinning Heel Kick? Practice them in turn and see where they differ and where they match.

Notes: Basically, the leg action for The Reverse Foot-Thrust is similar to The Sideways Foot-Thrust. However, whereas The Sideways Foot-Thrust requires the body just to be twisted sideways-on to the opponent, The Reverse Foot-Thrust necessitates an actual half-turn. Using the lead foot is a more advanced technique as it involves taking a step forwards first to change your stance.

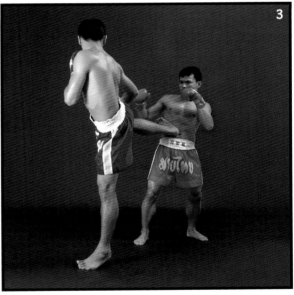

 3. Then, while transferring your body-weight to your left leg, pull your right leg up and into your body, with your knee bent and your heel pointing towards the target.

 4. Extending your right leg from the hip in a continuous line, thrust the sole of your foot against the target.

4. The Slapping Foot-Thrust

Thai: ถีบตบ - *Teeb Dhob*

Targets: Face, collar-bone

Focus: The leg is extended straight out to the front and raised high in the air, then slammed downwards, slapping against the target in passing.

S t e p   b y   S t e p

Notes: The rear foot is almost invariably used for this technique.

Hint: Some more detective work! Compare this with The Axe Heel Kick (pp.228-9) and spot the differences and similarities for yourself

Rear Slapping Foot-Thrust

1. Center your body-weight on your left leg and go up onto the ball of your left foot as you raise your right leg straight and high in the air, toes pointing upwards. Your right arm should be extended in order to stabilize the body.

2. Slam your right foot vertically downwards to slap against the target.

5. The Jumping Foot-Thrust

Thai: กระโดดถีบ - *Gra-dode Teeb*

Targets: Face, chin, neck chest, solar plexus, abdomen

Focus: Use both feet to spring off the ground, then thrust one foot against the target while in mid-air.

Step by Step

 Jump + Rear Straight Foot-Thrust

 1. Bend your knees in readiness for the spring.

Variations: The Straight Foot-Thrust and The Sideways Foot-Thrust are commonly utilized in combination with this jump.

Notes: This is a powerful technique because of the combined forces of the jump and the foot-thrust itself. It can have even greater power if it is used while your opponent is moving in towards you. The rear foot is generally used for this technique, being the more powerful.

Reminder: You have the absolute minimum of time to prepare your attack once you are in mid-air. So practice until you can co-ordinate the movements instinctively.

2. Using both feet, spring into the air, extending your right arm out and down while maintaining your left arm in its protective position. Bring your right leg up in readiness to thrust against the opponent, while your left leg begins to extend downwards in preparation for landing.

3. As your straightened left leg nears the floor, extend your right leg forwards and thrust your foot against the target, utilizing The Straight Foot-Thrust technique.

CHAPTER

Basic Plus

Once you have mastered the range of basic techniques outlined so far, for a little extra effort and determination you can add a touch of flair and polish to your Muay Thai in two ways: up-grade your basic arsenal and incorporate blocking and avoiding techniques into your offensive style.

Covering all five basic Muay Thai techniques, this chapter shows how you can use combination attacks, deceptive moves and a variety of couplings to enable you to achieve more effective results. It also describes eight easily accessible blocking techniques and a pair of simple methods to help you avoid an offensive move.

Once again, photographs of the Muay Thai stance are provided each time, with written details only if you need to pay special attention to some particular circumstances or if there is some deviation from the norm.

Punch Plus Up-

1. The One-Two Punch

Focus: This uses the combination of The Jab immediately followed by The Cross.

Notes: A very popular and commonly used Muay Thai combination

Step by Step

1. Strike out with The Jab, making your opponent believe that this is your main attack.

2. Then surprise them by following on with The Cross, which is your real attack. When deployed in this way, The Cross is more powerful than used on its own, as you can put extra "twist" behind the punch.

Grading
the Muay Thai Arsenal

Stance

2. Deflect and Punch

Focus: First knock away an opponent's punch with your right fist and then land a punch of your own with your left.

Notes: The photos show The Jab being used: this is a quick and effective choice. The Hook is a more advanced alternative.

Step by Step

1. Use your rear fist to deftly deflect your opponent's attempted punch.

2. Then, before your opponent can move out of range, quickly follow through with The Jab, twisting your body round and forwards to increase its power.

3. Step and Spin

Focus: Make your opponent believe that you are going to use a basic lead fist punch, but then add a spin and surprise them with a version of The Spinning Back Fist.

Notes: You need to be at some distance from your opponent to use this technique.

Step by Step

1. Step forwards with your right foot, then pivot on your right foot, bringing your left foot round...

2. ...in a clockwise half-circle so that you have your back towards your opponent. Don't forget to quickly turn your head so that you can nevertheless see your opponent over your left shoulder.

3. Using the ball of your right foot as the pivot turn counter-clockwise, twisting your left shoulder, hip and leg over to the left as you lash out with the back of your left fist against the side of your opponent's face.

Elbow Plus

1. Elbow Counter-Attack

Focus: The opponent's plan to deploy a knee-kick is thwarted by a timely attack with The Forward Elbow Thrust.

Stance

Step by Step
As your opponent attempts to grasp your neck with both hands in readiness to deploy a knee-kick, quickly move your left foot forwards and, with your right foot braced against the ground, destroy their offensive by striking their chin /face with your left elbow in The Forward Elbow Thrust technique.

2. Neck Grasp + Elbow

Focus: By grasping the opponent's neck you trick them into believing you are going to deploy a knee-kick, but instead you strike your elbow against their jaw.

Step by Step

1. In the Muay Thai stance, lean slightly forwards and grasp your opponent's neck with both hands as if you are going to use a knee-kick.

2. However, instead of that, take your opponent by surprise by using the ball of your right foot as the pivot to twist your left shoulder and hip over to the right and bring your left elbow diagonally upwards against your opponent's jaw in The Uppercut Elbow technique.

Stance

3. Elbow+Elbow

Focus: An offensive with the rear elbow is followed immediately by the deployment of the lead elbow.

1

Step by Step
1. Pivoting to the left on the ball of your left foot and slipping your right foot round to the front, use your right arm in The Horizontal Elbow technique to strike your opponent's right upper-arm as they attempt to deploy The Cross

2

2. Pivoting on your left foot, turn counter-clockwise so that you have your back to your opponent. The heels of both your feet are pointing to the revised target as you raise your bent left elbow out to the side in readiness. Of course, you have turned your head so that you can observe your opponent over your left shoulder!

3

3. Finally, complete the sequence by twisting your left shoulder and hip round to the left as you strike your opponent on the jaw with The Spinning Elbow.

4. The Jab + The Horizontal Elbow

Focus: Follow up The Jab quickly with The Lead Horizontal Elbow, using first the fist and then the elbow of the left arm.

S t e p   b y   S t e p

1. Hit out with The Jab to your opponent's chin, sliding your left foot (*seub tao*) further forwards as you do so.

2. Before your opponent has time to respond, bringing your rear foot a little further to the front and leaning forwards, bend your left elbow and strike your opponent's jaw a second time using The Horizontal Elbow technique.

Knee Plus

1. Counter-Attacking Knee-Kick

Focus: The opponent's attempts to land a kick are countered by a knee-kick.

Notes: This is an extremely dangerous combination which is easily capable of breaking the opponent's leg when deployed by a skilled Muay Thai fighter.

Stance

Step by Step
As the opponent tries to strike your left thigh or left side of your trunk with their right foot (The Low Round or The Middle Round respectively), you quickly counter by going fully up onto the ball of your left foot, which skids forwards as you lean backwards and, twisting your right hip, swing your right knee diagonally upwards to strike the inside of your opponent's right thigh in The Knee Bomb technique.

2. Waist Grapple + Knee-Kick

Focus: The opponent's plans to grasp your neck and deploy a knee-kick are destroyed as you grapple their waist and land a knee-kick yourself.

Notes: Although it is the neck which is usually grasped prior to using a knee-kick, grappling the opponent's waist is, in fact, even more effective.

Step by Step

1. As the opponent comes in close to grasp your neck, intending to then use a knee-kick, you quickly destroy the plan by grappling their waist, ensuring that your arms are inside theirs if at all possible (i.e. following the same basic rule as for grasping the neck.)

2. Then raise your right knee and deploy The Knee Slap on the left side of the opponent's trunk.

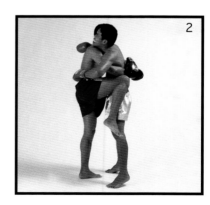

3. Shake + Knee-Kick

Focus: The opponent's neck is grasped in the normal way and then shaken from side to side to unbalance them before striking them with your knee.

Notes: Steps 1 and 4 are the basic form; Steps 2 and 3 are the plus-factor shakes.

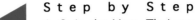

S t e p   b y   S t e p
1+2. In the Muay Thai stance, grasp your opponent's neck from the inside. Then, using the advantage the inside grip gives you, shake their neck to the right...

3. ...and then to the left...

4. ...before forcing them over to the right once more as, using the ball of your left leg as the pivot, with a twist of your right hip you swing your right knee diagonally upwards against your opponent's waist (The Diagonal Knee-Kick)

3. Avoidance + Knee-Kick

Focus: After avoiding the opponent's punch, The Knee Bomb is swung against the throat.

Notes: Although the hands are usually not used to grasp the opponent's neck in The Knee Bomb technique, in this case, given the level to which the knee is being raised, the right hand is used to ensure stability and pull the neck onto the knee.

Step by Step

1. Lean to your left in order to avoid the opponent's attempt to land The Cross and then swiftly extend your right arm, little finger uppermost, to grasp the back of the opponent's neck.

2. As the momentum of the failed punch is still taking the opponent forwards, pivot on the ball of your left foot as you twist your right hip and lean well over to the left, pulling on the back of the opponent's neck while you thrust your right knee in The Knee Bomb technique against the opponent's throat.

Kick Plus

1. The Low Round + Press

Focus: The shin impacts the front of the opponent's thighs in the Low Round Kick and then is maintained in this position.

Notes: Although this combination is often used, it requires skill and daring, because it involves being very close to the opponent and quick decision-making. It is capable of inflicting a great deal of pain on the opponent.

Step by Step

1. In the Muay Thai stance, you notice that your opponent is in the left-handed stance (i.e. they are actually left-handed or have taken a step forwards with their right foot from the right-handed stance. Whichever is the case, it is essential that you and your opponent are in contrasting stances).

2. Straightening your right arm in a natural way, swing your lower right leg, bent at the knee, in The Low Round so that your shin impacts the front of both your opponent's thighs and then is maintained pressed against them.

2. Neck Grasp + The Low Round to the Outer Knee

Focus: The right fist is extended to grasp the opponent's neck and force it over and downwards while the right leg kicks forwards with The Low Round to the Outer Knee

S t e p   b y   S t e p
1. Extend your right arm and grasp the right side of your opponent's neck with your little finger uppermost.

2. In a dual action, pull your opponent's neck over and downwards, while you swing your right leg up and forwards to impact your shin against the back of the opponent's left knee.

3. Knee-Kick Preparation + The Diagonal Kick

Focus: The opponent is deceived into expecting a knee-kick and then is struck by The Diagonal Kick.

Step by Step

1. Put all your body-weight on your right leg as you raise your left foot onto the ball, bending the knee, as if in preparation for a knee-kick. Complete the deception by actually lifting the knee straight up.

2. Then, taking your opponent completely by surprise, straighten your leg and lash your instep against their neck or jaw in The Diagonal Kick.

1. Miss the Target +
The Spinning Heel Kick

Focus: After a kick with the rear foot accidentally or deliberately misses the target, the momentum of the failed kick is used to continue turning and lash out with the lead foot in The Spinning Heel Kick.

Step by Step

1. The opponent leans back so your offensive with The Rear High Round, misses the target.

2. The momentum of your missed kick carries you round to the rear, with your back to the opponent, who, thinking that you are off-balance, comes in to make their own offensive move.

Notes: Speed -- both physical and mental -- is of the utmost importance in this combination: decisions have to be made quickly and then implemented without delay.

Variations: At Step 3, alternative possibilities are The Spinning Elbow or The Spinning Back Fist

3. However, you use the momentum to your advantage: transferring your body-weight to your right foot, you continue turning counter-clockwise.

4. Then, leaning over to the right, start to raise your left leg.

5. Pivoting further round on your right foot, your left foot lashes out against the target.

Foot-Thrust Plus

1. Opponent's Kick + Foot-Thrust

Focus: React to the opponent's kicking offensive by blocking it with a foot-thrust.

Notes: The usual defensive response to a kick is to block it with the knee. To use a foot-thrust in this situation requires more skill -- but it is less painful!

Stance

Step by Step

As your opponent starts to swing The Low Round Kick with their rear foot, use the sole of your lead foot to thrust against their lower thigh (just above the knee).

1

2. The Low Round to the Inner Knee + The Straight Foot-Thrust

Focus: After attacking with The Low Round to the Inner Knee, progress immediately to The Straight Foot-Thrust without lowering the leg in between.

Notes: This is a combination favored by exponents of Muay Thai who are skillful at both kicking and foot-thrusting.

S t e p   b y   S t e p

1. With your body-weight on your rear leg, use your lead leg to swing The Low Round against your opponent's left inner knee.

2. Then, without lowering your leg, pivot round to the left on your right foot, twisting your left hip back to the left, and thrust forwards in The Straight Foot-Thrust, using the ball of your foot to impact against your opponent's abdomen.

3. The Diagonal Kick +
The Sideways Foot-Thrust

Focus: After The Diagonal Kick fails to reach the target (Step 1), continue the offensive with The Sideways Foot-Thrust (Steps 2, 3 & 4).

Variations: After Step 1, a range of other options are possible, including The Spinning Heel Kick.

Step by Step
1. Using your right foot as the pivot, swing you left leg upwards in The Diagonal Kick, aiming to hit the opponent's upper body. However, they successfully avoid your kick.

2. Carried round by the momentum of the failed kick, you now have your back to the opponent. Remember to observe them closely over your left shoulder!

3. Still using your right leg as the pivot, start to raise your left leg, bending it at the knee, as you lean over to the right.

4. Thrust your leg out in The Sideways Foot-Thrust to impact the ball of your left foot against your opponent's solar plexus.

Blocking and Avoiding

To state the obvious, if you want to become proficient in Muay Thai, you need to develop defensive as well as attacking skills. In this section, you will find a range of basic blocking and avoiding techniques which you should easily be able to incorporate into your work-out. All the techniques start from the Muay Thai stance.

1. Simultaneously lift your shoulders, tuck your chin in and raise both fists in front of your face to protect your head and neck from a punch.

Stance

2. Use both your lower arms to block your opponent's kick to the middle of your body.

3. Leaning forwards, extend both your arms straight out to block a punch and then follow this on with either a kick or a knee-kick. Both this technique and Number 4 are generally used by fighters who are themselves weak at punching.

4. Take a short step forwards with your left foot, lean your body forwards, right arm bent protectively, fist by your jaw to move from the main focus of your opponent's kick and block it, extend your left arm to knock them off-balance.

N.B. When using technique No5 you should take great care to:

a. use the upper part of your shin, as the bone is bigger
b. use the front of your shin: using the side could be very painful.

5. Without changing the relative positions of your head, shoulders, trunk and arms from the Muay Thai stance in any way, twist to the left and raise your left leg, bent at the knee, using the upper part of your shin to block your opponent's attack with the Rear Low Round to the Outer Knee.

6. Using the same method as No.5, block your opponent's attack as they use their lead leg in The Low Round to the Inner Knee technique.

7. Pivoting to your left on your right foot, raise your bent left knee higher than in No.5 and 6 and use it to block your opponent's attack with The Rear Middle Round

Tip: Although knee blocks are very effective, it should be noted that they are only applicable to attacks targeting the lower and central regions of the body.

Stance

8. Pivoting to your right on your right foot, raise your left knee as in No.7 and use it to block The Middle Round which your opponent is extending, this time with their lead foot.

Stance

9. Keeping your feet in their basic Muay Thai stance positions, lean your trunk backwards while keeping your neck and head vertical to avoid your opponent's attack with The Rear High Round. You can then easily counter-attack.

Stance

10. As your opponent swings their right foot at you in The Middle Round, avoid it by pulling your feet backwards and pulling in your stomach and hips, so that your body is arched over, your arms stretched forwards over your bent head.

Appendix A
Map Showing Places Referred to in the Text

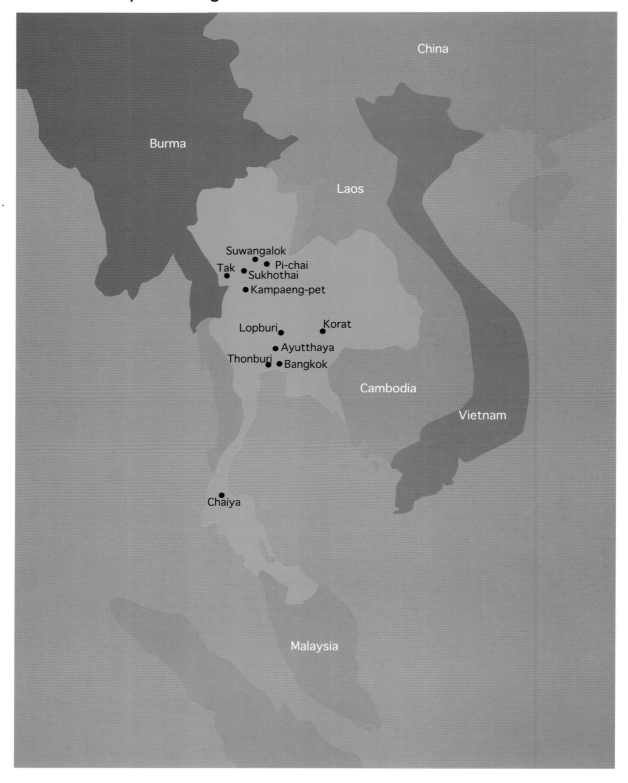

Direction in which Weapons are Impacted Against the Target

Weapon / Direction	Punch	Elbow Strike	Knee-Kick	Kick	Foot-Thrust
Vertical: Upwards	Uppercut	–	Straight Knee-Kick	Straight Kick / Nutcracker Kick	–
Vertical: Downwards	–	Elbow Chop / Double Elbow Chop	–	Axe Heel Kick	Slapping Foot-Thrust
Horizontal: Inwards	–	Horizontal Elbow	Horizontal Knee-Kick / Slapping Knee-Kick	Round Kick	–
Horizontal: Outwards	Spinning Back Fist	Reverse Horizontal Elbow / Spinning Elbow	–	Spinning Heel Kick	–
Horizontal: Forwards	Straight Punch / Jump Punch	Forward Elbow-Thrust	Flying Knee-Kick / Step-Up Knee-Kick	Straight Foot-Thrust / Sideways Foot-Thrust / Reverse Foot-Thrust / Jumping Foot-Thrust	Half-Shin, Half Knee Kick / Step-Up Kick
Diagonal: Upwards	–	Uppercut Elbow	Diagonal Knee-Kick / Knee Bomb	Diagonal Kick	–
Diagonal: Downwards	–	Elbow Slash	–	–	–
Curving: Sideways	Hook / Swing	–	–	–	–
Curving: Over+Down	Overhead Punch	–	Curving Knee-Kick	Down Round Kick	–

Appendix C

Position & Function of Parts of the Body when Attacking

Weapon / Part of the body	Head & Neck	Arms	Shoulders	Trunk & Hips	Knees	Feet
Punch	Inclined slightly forwards, chin tucked in. Twisted to look over shoulder in The Spinning Back Fist.	One arm extended in the punch. Other arm held protectively, fist by the chin, elbow at the waist.	Twisted to add power to the punch.	Twisted to add power to the punch.	Sometimes bent and then follows action of hips and feet.	Used as the pivot.
Elbow Strike	Held slightly forwards. Twisted to look over shoulder in the Reverse Horizontal Elbow and The Spinning Elbow.	Elbow of one arm used offensively. Other arm held protectively, fist by the chin, elbow at the waist.	Used as pivot for swinging elbow and to put extra force behind it.	Twisted to add power to the elbow.	Moved naturally along with trunk and feet	Used as the pivot.
Knee-Kick	Head inclined with chin tucked into base of the throat.	One or both hands usually used to grasp opponent's neck.	Held naturally.	Twisted to add power to the knee.	Thrust upwards, forwards or round against the target.	One foot used as the pivot and braced against the floor for extra thrust.
Kick	Usually slightly inclined with chin tucked in. Twisted to look over shoulder in The Spinning Heel Kick.	Both held in defensive position or, more naturally one held defensively and the other swung out for extra power	Held naturally.	Twisted along with the kick.	Knee of attacking leg raised and bent in preparation for kicking.	One foot used to kick. Other foot used as the pivot.
Foot-Thrust	Head inclined, chin tucked in. Twisted to look over shoulder in The Reverse Foot-Thrust.	Both held in defensive position or, more naturally one held defensively and the other swung out for extra power	Held naturally	Hip on attacking side used to add power to foot.	Knee of attacking leg raised and bent in preparation for thrusting, then extended.	Ball (80 % of time) or toes, sole, heel used to thrust against the target

Thai-English
Glossary

The following is a list of Thai words which occur in this volume and their English meaning. It should be noted that, unlike some languages which have their own script, there is no officially accepted way to transcribe Thai using the roman alphabet. Readers must therefore expect to encounter variant forms of transcription in other books they may consult. Although "th" and "ph" are commonly used to transcribe certain aspirated consonants, these are not used in this book in order to avoid confusion with the English pronunciation of these combinations. (An exception to this is where they occur in place names like "Ayutthaya", the spelling of which has become virtually standardized). "Dh" has been used to transcribe a sound which does not exist in English and which can best be reproduced by pushing the tongue hard against the front part of the roof of the mouth whilst pronouncing a normal "d". In this way, the English "dad" becomes transformed into the Thai "dhad", meaning "cut". Unfortunately, as there is no method of indicating the five tones which occur in spoken Thai and also no accurate way of transcribing the language's complex vowel sounds, the best that can be achieved is an approximation.

A

ajarn   - อาจารย์ teacher, instructor etc. (cf. *khru*)

arwud   - อาวุธ weapons

B

bae mue   - แบมือ sliding both hands out to the side during a prostration of respect

bon   - บน upper, top, above

boran   - โบราณ old, ancient

Buwong Suwong   - บวงสรวง Informing the Spirits Ceremony, a Brahmin rite

C

ching   - ฉิ่ง small Thai cymbals used to provide rhythm

chiyang   - เฉียง diagonal

D

dern   - เดิน walk

dhaam   - ตาม follow

dhad   - ตัด cut

dhagrut   - ตะกรุด a kind of amulet made from beaten bronze or silver

dhagrut puong   - ตะกรุดพวง a cluster of *dhagrut*

dhagrut tone   - ตะกรุดโทน a single *dhagrut*

Dhamruot Luang   - ตำรวจหลวง the "royal police" of the Ayutthaya period

dhe   - เตะ kick

dhee kow   - ตีเข่า method of using the knee offensively

Dhee Muay   - ตีมวย ancient form of muay

dhee sork   - ตีศอก method of using the elbow offensively

dhob   - ตบ slap, hit

Dhoi Muay   - ต่อยมวย alternative for *Dhee Muay* (q.v.)

dhrong   - ตรง straight, direct

F

fun kow   - ฟันเข่า alternative for *dhee kow* (q.v.)

279

fun sork	- ฟันศอก alternative for *dhee sork* (q.v.)

G

gamrai pirod	- กำไรพิรอด bracelet form of *pirod* (q.v.)
gao	- เก้า step forwards, advance
glab lang	- กลับหลัง turn to the back
glang	- กลาง center, middle
glong kaek	- กลองแขก one of a pair of drums used by the *wong pee glong* (q.v.)
gon hoi	- ก้นหอย whorl, spiral; the protrusions on the back of the knuckles bound in the *kaad chuek* (q.v.)
Gong Tanai Luak	- กองทนายเลือก alternative name for the *Dhamruot Luang* (q.v.)
gra-dode	- กระโดด jump, leap
gra-jap	- กระจับ groin-protector, "the box"
Grom Nak Muay	- กรมนักมวย alternative name for the *Dhamruot Luang* (q.v.)
gung gaeng khaa guay	- กางเกงขาก๊วย traditional knee-length baggy pants, worn by *muay* fighters in the past

H

hang	- หาง tail

J

jarot muay	- จรดมวย the Muay Thai stance
jerakhae	- จระเข้ crocodile
jerm	- เจิม the custom of marking three dots on the forehead with powder to bring good fortune
jongrabein	- โจงกระเบน pantaloons fashioned from *paa-nung* (q.v.) and worn by *muay* fighters in the past
jot muay	- จดมวย alternative for *jarot muay* (q.v.)

jot muay liem khwaa	- จดมวยเหลี่ยมขวา the Muay Thai stance for a right-handed fighter
jot muay liem sai	- จดมวยเหลี่ยมซ้าย the Muay Thai stance for a left-handed fighter

K

kaad chuek	- คาดเชือก fist bindings used in the past
kaeng	- แข้ง shin
kang	- ข้าง side
kartar arkom	- คาถาอาคม incantations used for protection and strength
khai muay	- ค่ายมวย Muay Thai training camp
khouk	- โขก hitting
khru	- ครู teacher, instructor
khru muay	- ครูมวย Muay Thai teacher
khwaa	- ขวา right
koo	- คู่ pair
kow	- เข่า knee
krabi krabong	- กระบี่กระบอง Thai swordplay
Krob Khru	- ครอบครู the elevating of a Muay Thai fighter to the rank of *khru muay* (q.v.)
krueng rang korng klang krueng sakkara	- เครื่องรางของขลัง amulets
buchaa khru	- เครื่องสักการะบูชาครู symbols of respect given in homage to a teacher
krueng	- ครึ่ง half
Kuen Khru	- ขึ้นครู the acceptance of a fighter by a *khru muay* (q.v.) as his student
Kuen Suu Weitee	- ขึ้นสู่เวที approaching the ring

L

laang	- ล่าง bottom, lower
lang	- หลัง back, rear, behind
lang mud	- หลังหมัด the back of the fist

loy	- ลอย flying, floating	*paa-nung*	- ผ้านุ่ง rectangular piece of cloth wrapped around the lower part of the body and worn as an everyday garment in the past
Luk Len	- ลูกเล่น the Dramatic Interlude in the *Wai Khru Ram Muay*		

M

mongkon	- มงคล head circlet worn by a Muay Thai fighter but removed before the actual contest	*paa-yan*	- ผ้ายันต์ amulet consisting of a cloth inscribed with a mystical number
		pee	- ปี year
Muay Boran	- มวยโบราณ ancient form of *muay* as preserved and practiced today	*pee chawaa*	- ปี่ฉวา Javanese oboe played to accompany Muay Thai rituals and bouts
mud	- หมัด fist	*panom mue*	- พนมมือ posture involving holding the hands, palms together, at chest-level
mud dhaam	- หมัดตาม the rear fist		
mud lang	- หมัดหลัง alternative for *mud dhaam* (q.v.)		
mud naa	- หมัดหน้า the lead fist	*panom mue wai*	- พนมมือไหว้ gesture of respect combining the *panom mue* posture (q.v.) and bowing the head
mud nam	- หมัดนำ alternative for *mud naa* (q.v.)		
muen	- หมื่น an honorific title the equivalent of a knighthood	*pitsamorn*	- พิศมร amulet traditionally made from a palm leaf
		pirod	- พิรอด amulet fashioned from rattan (cf. *gamrai pirod* and *wehn pirod*)

N

naa	- หน้า front	*pitee*	- พิธี ceremony, used in combinations such as *Pitee Kuen Khru, Pitee Krob Khru* etc to indicate the actual ceremony rather than its specific contents
naakhaa	- นาคา dragon or giant serpent of Thai mythology		
nai	- นาย Mr.		
nak muay	- นักมวย Muay Thai fighter		
nam	- นำ front, leading		
na-wa arwud	- นวอาวุธ the original "Nine Weapons" of *muay*, i.e. head, fists, elbows, knees, feet	*pra*	- พระ honorific title equivalent of a lord
		prachao	- พระเจ้า king
		prajam	- ประจำ regular

P

paa pan mue	- ผ้าพันมือ hand-wraps used by Muay Thai fighters under their gloves	*prajied*	- ประเจียด amulets tied around the fighter's upper arms and worn during a contest
paa-kao-maa	- ผ้าขาวม้า rectangular piece of cloth used by *muay* fighters in the past to secure their baggy pants at the waist and also to pad the genital area	*pra krueng*	- พระเครื่อง small Buddha image carried as an amulet
		praya	- พระยา honorific title the equivalent of count
		Prom See Naa	- พรหมสี่หน้า The Four Directions Sequence in the *Wai Khru Ram Muay*

R

radap	- ระดับ level
rook	- รุก forwards

S

saam	- สาม three
sai	- ซ้าย left
salap	- สลับ exchange, alternating
san mud	- สันหมัด back of the knuckles
sanam muay	- สนามมวย Muay Thai arena of the 1920-30s
sap	- สับ chop
see	- สี่ four
shok	- ชก punch
somdet prachao	- สมเด็จพระเจ้า king
soong	- สูง high, tall
sork	- ศอก elbow
sorn	- ศร arrow
suea yan	- เสื้อยันต์ amulet consisting of a waistcoat-type garment inscribed with mystical numbers
sueb	- สืบ continuous, following
suer	- เสือ tiger

T

Taa Prom Nang	- แทงเข่า The Kneeling Sequence of the *Wai Khru Ram Muay*
taeng	- แทง stab, pierce
taeng kow	- แทงเข่า alternative for *dhee kow* (q.v.)
tao	- เท้า foot
tao dhaam	- เท้าตาม the rear foot
tao lang	- เท้าหลัง alternative for *tao dhaam* (q.v.)
tao naa	- เท้าหน้า the lead foot
tao nam	- เท้านำ alternative for *tao naa* (q.v.)
Tawai Bangkom	- ถวายบังคม The Royal Homage Sequence in the *Wai Khru Ram Muay*
teeb	- ถีบ foot-thrust
tod mongkon	- ถอดมงคล removal of the head circlet
toi	- ถอย backwards

W

Waad Mue or *Waad Kaen*	- วาดมือ หรือ วาดแขนThe Out stretched Arms sequence in the *Wai Khru Ram Muay*
waahn	- ว่าน herb given mystical properties by passing through an incantation ritual
wai	- ไหว้ raising the hands, palms together, in a gesture of respect
Wai Khru Prajam Pee	- ไหว้ครูประจำปี the annual paying of homage to teachers
Wai Khru Ram Muay	- ไหว้ครูรำมวย ritual dance of homage performed by a fighter before the commencement of a bout and on other occasions
Wan Khru	- วันครู teacher's day, Thursday
Wan Muay Thai	- วันมวยไทย Muay Thai Day, 17th March
wat	- วัด temple
wehn pirod	- แหวนพิรอด ring made from *pirod* (q.v.) and worn as an amulet
weitee	- เวที ring, stage, platform
weitee muay	- เวทีมวย the Muay Thai ring
wiyang	- เหวี่ยง swerving, curving
wong pee glong	- วงปี่กลอง group of four musicians who provide the accompaniment for Muay Thai

Y

yao	- ยาว long
yiep	- เหยียบ step on
yok	- ยก lift, raise, elevate
Yok Khru	- ยกครู alternative for *Kuen Khru* (q.v.)

Index

A

Aer Muong Dee 42
Alternating Stance Footwork 132
amulets
    belief in 61, 68
    dhagrut 68, 69
    mongkon 61, 70
    obligatory items 61, 68
    paa-yan 70
    pra krueng 69
    pirod 69
    pitsamorn 69
    prajied 69
    suea yan 70
    used by amateurs 67
    used by professionals 65
    used in the past 63
    used by women 92
    waahn 69
Ancient *Muay* 33
animism 78
Annual Homage-Paying Ceremony 75, 83
Approaching the Ring Rites 96-9
arenas
    Lak Muang 55, 56
    Suan Gularb 21, 39, 54
    Suan Jao Ched 55, 56
    Suan Sanuk 55, 56
    Tar Chang 55, 56
    Tar Prachan 56
avoidance techniques 275
Axe Heel Kick 228-9
Ayutthaya 19, 28, 50, 51, 52, 62

B

blocking techniques 272-5
Bound Fist *Muay* 24
Buwong Suwong 78-9
Boxing Skip 138
Bruce Lee 45
Buddhism 15, 17, 18, 76, 78

C

ceremonies
    Buwong Suwong 78-9
    Kuen Khru or *Yok Khru* 80
    Krob Khru 84-7
    Wai Khru Prajam Pee 83
Chaiya 18, 35, 37

ching 94
Close Quarters Round Kick 188-91
"Coiled Dragon's Tail" 226-7
Crash Kick 228-9
"Crocodile Tail Thrash" 224
Cross 146-7, 252, 257, 262
Curving Knee-Kick 188-91
cymbals 94

D

dhagrut 64, 69
dhamruot luang 28
dhe 206-33
Dhe Chiyang 220-1
Dhe Dhad 212-9
Dhe Dhrong 208-9
Dhe Faad 226-7
Dhe Glab Lang 224-5
Dhe Khouk 228-9
Dhe Kod 226-7
Dhe Krueng Khaeng, Krueng Kow 222-3
Dhe Paa Maak 210-1
Dhe Rid 220-1
dhee kow 180-205
Dhee Muay 23
dhee sork 150-79
Dhen 138
Dhoi Muay 23
Diagonal Footwork 134-5
Diagonal Kick 220-1, 265, 270
Diagonal Knee-Kick 186-7, 261
Double Elbow Chop 176-7
Down Round Kick 226-7
Dramatic Interlude *WKRM* poster*
drum 95

E

Elbow Chop 174-5
Elbow Plus 256-8
Elbow Slash 162-3
elbow strike 160-79
Elite Retainers 28

F

"Father of Muay Thai" 51
First Aid 122-3
fist 144
    method of binding (past) 24-5
    method of binding (present) 115-7

Index

method of clenching 114
fist bindings 115
composition of 24
addition of *gon hoi* 24
doctoring of 24
incantations and 24
Flying Knee-Kick 202-3
foot-thrusts 234-49
Foot-Thrust Plus 268-71
footwork 125-39
Forward Elbow Thrust 168-9, 255
Four Directions Sequence *WKRM* poster*
fun kow 180-205
fun sork 150-179

G

gamrai pirod 69
Gao Blien Liem 132
Gao Chaak 134-5
glong kaek 94, 95
gon hoi 24
Gong Tanai Luak 28
gloves, introduction of 40
Gra-dode 139
Gra-dode Dhe 230-1
Gra-dode Shok 156-7
Gra-dode Sork 178-9
Gra-dode Teeb 248-9
gra-jap 42
groin protector 42
Grom Nak Muay 28
gung gaeng khaa guay 63

H

Half-Shin, Half-Knee Kick 222-3
hand-wraps
application of 116-7
functions of 115
herbs 69
High Round Kick 212-3, 266, 275
Hook 148-9, 253
Horizontal Elbow 164-5, 257, 258
Horizontal Knee-Kick 192-5

I

incantations 61, 71
Indochina Peninsula 61, 71
Informing the Spirits Ceremony 78-9
Initiation as a Trainee Fighter Ceremony
75, 80
Initiation as a Teacher Ceremony 75, 84-7

J

Jab 146-7, 252, 253, 258
jarot muay 118
Javanese oboe 95, 95
Jee Chang 39
"Jerakhae Faad Hang" 224-5
jerm 83
Jia Kaegkhmen 40
jongrabein 62
jot muay 18
judo 141
Jump Kick 230-1
Jump Punch 157
Jumping Foot-Thrust 248-9

K

kaad chuek 16, 19, 24-5, 40, 55
"Kaeg Chao Sen" 95
Kammuey Muang Yod 40
karate 15, 141, 144, 160
kartar arkom 61, 71
Khru Kaet 37
khru muay 74
Khru Tong 37
kicks 206-33
kick-boxing 45
Kick Plus 263-7
Knee Bomb 200-1, 259, 262
Knee Glide 200-1
Knee Plus 259-62
Knee Slap 196-9, 260
knee-kicks 180-205
Kneeling Sequence *WKRM* poster*
knuckles 144
kow 180-205
Kow Chiyang 186-7
Kow Dhad 192-5
Kow Dhob 196-9
Kow Dhrong 184-5
Kow Kouwng 188-91
Kow Loy 202-3
Kow Yiep 204-5
Kow Youwn 200-1
Krob Khru 84
krueng rang korng klang 61
krueng sakkara buchaa khru 80

Index

Kuen Khru 80
Kuen Suu Weitee 96-9
kung-fu 45

L

lead fist 118-9, 144
lead foot 118-9
Leaping 139
Leg-Block Footwork 136-7
Low Round Kick 216-9, 259, 263, 264, 268, 269, 274
Luk Len WKRM poster*
Lumpini Stadium 21, 59, 92

M

Mae Mai Muay Thai 45
Mae Torrannee 96
Mangra, King 51
mavya 16
Mid-Air Elbow Attack 178-9
Middle Round Kick 214-5, 259, 274, 275
mongkon
    receiving of 87
    removal of 107
    Tod Mongkon 107
    tradition of 70
    women and 92
Muay Boran 33
    training methods of 46
    Yaang Saam Khum in 47
    Wai Khru Ram Muay and 47
Muay Chaiya 33, 34-7
Muay Fighters' Regiment 28
Muay Kaad Chuek 24, 33
Muay Korat 33, 39
Muay Luang 28
Muay Pra Nakorn 30, 37
Muay Shuffle 47, 126-131
Muay Thai
    ceremonies 73-87
    history of 13-59
    internationalization of 21, 40-5
    origins of 16-7
    outfit 62-7
    religion and 17
    traditions of 73-87
    weapons 141-249
Muay Thai Day 51, 83
Muay Thai fighter

amateur 64-5
    outfit of 64-7
    professional 66-7
    training of 42
Muay Thai Stance 118-9
mud dhaam or *mud lang* 119, 144
Mud Dhrong 146-7
Mud Khouk 158-9
mud naa or *mud nam* 119, 144
Mud Soy Dow 154-5
Mud Suey 154-5
Mud Wiyang Glab 152-3
Mud Wiyang San 148-9
Mud Wiyang Yao 150-1
Muen Cha-ngad Choeng Shok 21, 30, 33
Muen Muay Mee Chue 21, 30, 33, 36, 37
Muen Mue Maen Mud 21, 30, 33
Muen Plaan 20, 53
music
    accompanying the fight 94-5
    accompanying the *Wai Khru Ram Muay* 94-5
    instruments 94-5
    "*Kaeg Chao Sen*" 95
    "*Salamaa*" 95
    tempo of 95

N

"*Naakhaa Khanod Hang*" 226-7
na-wa arwud 141
Nai Khanom Tom 19, 51, 62
Nin Paksee 37
Noguchi, Osamu 45
Nop Chom Sri Maek 40
Nutcracker Kick 210-1

O

Olympics 48
outfit
    amateur 66-7
    professional 64-5
    traditional 62-3
Outstretched Arms *WKRM* poster*
Overhead Punch 158-9

P

paa-kao-maa 63
paa-nung 62
paa-yan 68, 70

Index

Pae Lieng Prasert 40
panom mue 99
panom mue wai 87, 99, 107
Pattanagorn Theater 56
Paw-Tan Mar 37
Paying Respect to Teachers 73-87
pee chawaa 94, 95
pirod 69
    gamrai pirod 69
    wehn pirod 69
pitsamorn 69
Pitee Tod Mongkon 107
pra krueng 69
"Pra Ram Pleng Sorn" 104-5
Pra Chai Choke Shok Channa 21, 30
Prachao Taksin Maharaj 20, 52
prajied 16, 68, 69
Praya Pi-chai Dab Hak 20, 52
Praya Watjeesattayarak 37
preparatory stance
    adoption of 118-9
    for a left-handed fighter 118
    for a right-handed fighter 119
Prom See Naa WKRM poster*
Pum Riang 37
Punch Plus 252-5
punches 144-59

R

Rama V 21, 28, 30, 33, 54
Rama VI 21, 28, 30, 39
Ratchadamnoen Stadium 21, 58, 92
Rattanakosin 20-1
rear fist 118-9, 144
rear foot 118-9
Removal of the Head Circlet 107
Reverse Elbow 170-1
Reverse Foot-Thrust 244-5
ring
    entering 96-9
    superstitions and 90
    women and 92
ring name 90
Ritual Dance of Homage 75, 83, 87, 101-5
    Kneeling Sequence 105
    Royal Homage Sequence 105
    Standing Sequence 105
rituals
    jerm 83

Kuen Suu Weitee 96-9
Pre-Contest 89-107
Tod Mongkon 107
Wai Khru Ram Muay 101-5
Round Kick 212-9
Royal Homage Sequence *WKRM* poster*
Royal *Muay* 28
Running-Jump Knee-Kick 202-3

S

"Salamaa" 95
Shaolin Temple 15
shok 144-59
Sideways Foot-Thrust 240-3, 270-1
Slapping Foot-Thrust 246-7
Somdet Prachao Suer 19, 50
sork 160-79
Sork Dhad 164-5
Sork Dhee 162-3
Sork Fun 162-3
Sork Glab 172-3
Sork Gratung 170-1
Sork Ngad 166-7
Sork Poong 168-9
Sork Sap 174-5
Sork Sap Koo 176-7
Sork Seuy 166-7
Sork Wiyang Glab 170-1
South East Asian Games 48
Spinning Back Fist 152-3, 254, 267
Spinning Elbow 172-3, 257, 267
Spinning Heel Kick 224-5, 266-7, 270
Sri Ayutthaya Theater 56
Srivijaya 18, 35
stadiums
    Lumpini 21, 59, 92
    Ratchadamnoen 21, 59, 91
"Star Gatherer" 154-5
Step-Slide Shuffle 133
Step-Up Kick 232-3
Step-Up Knee-Kick 204-5
Straight Foot-Thrust 236-9, 269
Straight Kick 208-9
Straight Knee-Kick 184-5
Straight Punch 146-7, 252
student
    respect for teacher 83
    acceptance by teacher 80
    becoming a teacher 84-7

Index

suea yan 70
Sueb Tao 133
"Suer Larg Hang" 36
Sukhothai 19
Sweeping Kick 212-9
Swing 150-1

T

Taa Prom Nang WKRM poster*
Tawai Bangkom WKRM poster*
taekwondo 15, 141, 144, 160
taeng kow 180-205
Taksin, King 20, 52
tao dhaam or *tao lang* 119
tao naa or *tao nam* 119
teacher
 elevation to 84
 paying respect to 83
 qualities of 75
 student being accepted by 80
 symbols of respect offered to 74
Teachers' Day 80
teeb 234-49
Teeb Dhob 246-7
Teeb Dhrong 236-9
Teeb Glab Lang 244-5
Teeb Jik 236-7
Teeb Kang 240-3
Teeb Neb 236-9
Teeb Soh 236-9
Teeb Tink 236-9
Teeb Yan 236-9
Thonburi 20, 52
Thonburi Theater 56
"Tiger Pulls the Tail" 36
Tod Mongkon 107
Tong Dee Fan Khao 52
traditions
 amulets 68-70
 incantations 71
 Krob Khru 84
 krueng sakkara buchaa khru 80
 Kuen Khru 80
 Kuen Suu Weitee 96-9
 music 94-9
 outfit 62-7
 Tod Mongon 107
 Wai Khru Prajam Pee 83
 Wai Khru Ram Muay 101-5

Yok Khru 80
training
 early methods 26
 developments 42

U

Uppercut 154-5
Uppercut Elbow 166-7, 256

V

vulnerable targets 120-1

W

Waad Kaen or *Waad Mue WKRM* poster*
waahn 69
wai 76-7
Wai Khru 73-87
Wai Khru Prajam Pee 83
Wai Khru Ram Muay
 Muay Boran and 47
 music for 95
 "Pra Ram Pleng Sorn" version 104-5
 prostrations in 103
 purpose of 102, 103
 ritual of 101-5
 Yaang Saam Khum in 105
warm-up exercises 110-3
weapons
 elbows 160-79
 feet 206-49
 fists 144-59
 knees 180-205
wehn pirod 69
women and Muay Thai 92
wong pee glong 94

Y

Yang Haan Talay 39
Yaang Saam Khum
 ceremonial form 105, 127
 details of 127-31
 fighting form 127
 in *Muay Boran* 47
 in *Wai Khru Ram Muay* 105
Yiep Dhe 232-3
Yok Khru 80
Yok Kow Bong-Gan 136-7

* Indicates an item to be found in the *Wai Khru Ram Muay* poster

Selected Bibliography

● I.M.P. 12th Anniversary, International Martial Arts Promotion, O.S. Printing House, Bangkok, 1990.

● Muay Thai: The King of Martial Arts, Rajadamnern Stadium Co., Ltd, Pholachai Printing Center Corp., Bangkok 1984.

● Muay Thai: The Most Distinguished Art of Fighting, Panya Kraitus, Dr. Pitisuk Kraitus, J. Film Process Co., Ltd Bangkok, 1988.

● อนุสรณ์ งานพระราชทานเพลิงศพ นายบุญยืน สุวรรณธาดา ยอดนักสู้ผู้เสียสละเพื่อ ศิลปะมวยไทย, บริษัทศิลป์สยามบรรจุภัณฑ์และการพิมพ์ จำกัด, กรุงเทพฯ, 1999.

● ตระกูล นวลมณี 84 ปี 7 รอบ นักษัตร, จำลองนวลมณี, 2001. มวยไทย - มวยสากล, ผู้ช่วยศาสตราจารย์จรวย แก่นวงษ์คำ, สำนักพิมพ์โอเดียนสโตร์, กรุงเทพฯ, 1987.

● ศิลปะมวยไทย, สำนักงานคณะกรรมการวัฒนธรรมแห่งชาติ, โรงพิมพ์คุรุสภา ลาดพร้าว, กรุงเทพฯ, 1997.

For your further information...

Readers considering coming to Thailand specifically to train in Muay Thai may like to consult the Directory provided at the www.muaythai.com web site. However, it should be stressed that the inclusion of a training center in the Directory does not constitute a recommendation by anyone involved in this book in any capacity. Readers should make their own detailed inquiries into all aspects of courses offered before coming to any decision.

It should be noted that Muay Thai Training Camps are generally for those intending to become professional fighters: the emphasis is on teaching essential fighting skills relatively quickly. On the other hand, gyms which have Muay Thai courses provide a broad-based introduction to the art, including its rituals and traditions. If you have a particularly strong interest in the historical and cultural aspects of muay, then you might like to consider training with a Muay Boran instructor.

The Muay Thai teachers who gave us so much of their valuable time and experience during the writing of this book - - Phitsanu Kusolwong, Chaichalerm Naksawart and Kridakom Sodprasert (Khru Lek) - -would be happy to give individual advice and can be contacted via Spry Books' dedicated Muay Thai e-mail hotline: muaythai@sprypublishing.com. All other related enquiries can also be sent to this address.

Photo Credits

Khru Tonglor Yarleh Collection

Khru Tonglor Yarleh (1930 - 1996) was an eminent and highly respected teacher of *Muay Chaiya* who devoted his life to the art of *muay*. He founded the *Pahuyut Chaiyarat* association to promote *Muay Boran*, in particular *Muay Chaiya*, and helped students at Chulalongkorn and Ramkamhaeng Universities to found Muay Thai societies. The photographs of *Khru* Tonglor featured in the volume were all taken in around 1990.

14 - 5   *Wai Khru*, *Muay Chaiya* style. *Khru* Tonglor is in a prostration pose known as *grarb ben-jarng-ka-pradit*, which involves touching the ground with 5 points of the body: the forehead, the palms of both hands and the elbows.

16 - 7   The *Suer Larg Hang* (Tiger Pulls the Tail) technique which is unique to *Muay Chaiya* (cf. p. 36)

34 - 5   *Muay Chaiya* stance

36   A posture known as *khon-khao-pra-su-mey-ru*, a name which derives from the *Ramakien*

37   *Wai Khru*, *Muay Chaiya* style

24 - 5   Two *Muay Chaiya* students of *Khru* Tonglor demonstrate a *Mae Mai Muay Thai* technique. The fighter on the left is using *Tat Mar-lar* ("Tucking a Flower Behind the Ear") to block his opponent's kick.

36   (bottom) In a recent photo, another student of *Khru* Tonglor, *Khru* Lek, demonstrates the stages of *Suer Larg Hang*

Historical Collection

22 - 3   Posed photograph of *muay*, from a series depicting everyday life of the Siamese taken in the reign of Rama V*

28 - 9   Posed studio photograph, again taken in the reign of Rama V*

30 - 1   *Muay* fighters displaying their skills in front of the king on 2nd December 1908 at the Sanpet Hall, Old Palace, Ayutthaya, as part of the festivities to celebrate Rama V's 40th Jubilee

39   A *muay* bout at the Suan Gularb Arena in the reign of Rama VI. An unverifiable tradition has it that the featured fighters are Jee Chang (left) and Yang Harn Talay (right) (cf.p.38-9). What can be said for certain is that the fighter on the left is not adopting a recogniz able *muay* technique.

40   A bout between, on the left, Lom Sasibud (*Muay Thonburi*) and Bud Somchard (*Muay Pra Nakorn*). Date and location unknown, possibly in a converted movie theater.

Past Greats Collection

All these photos were taken in the 1970s.

40 - 1   Sing Su-ra-garn uses the High Round to kick the temples of Tanong Lolita

42 - 3   Main photo: "The Crocodile Tail Thrash"
Top left: Low Round to the Inner Knee
Bottom Left: The Jab

44   The Elbow Slash

45   Both fighters featured on this page are left-handed
Top: Jump Kick
Bottom: Jump Kick

International *Wai Khru* Collection

71, 82-3, 84-5, 86-7
All these photos were taken at the International Muay Thai & Krabi Krabong *Wai Khru* Ceremony, held in Ayutthaya on 15th March 2001.

Miscellaneous

21 - 2   Night scenes in Bangkok: (from left the right)
The Temple of the Dawn as seen from the Chao Praya River
The Temple of the Dawn
The Temple of the Emerald Buddha
The modern city

26 - 7   Gongiet Parsukgun, wearing a traditional *muay* outfit, demonstrates 4 training methods from the past:
Targeting the trunk of a banana tree for kicking practice
Chopping water in the river to develop unblinking focus
Using a suspended lime for eye-sight and avoidance practice
Punching practice using coconuts floating in the river

51   Memorial statue to *Nai* Khanom Tom, Ayutthaya Provincial Sports Ground

52   Memorial statue to *Praya* Pi-chai Dab Hak, Utaradit

53   View of Wat Pra Kaew and the Grand Palace where *Muen* Plaan fought with the French brothers

78   Salvers of auspicious offerings to the spirits formed from woven banana leaves and featuring marigolds

81   *Krueng Sakkara Buchaa Khru*: the symbols of respect - - lotus flowers, candles and incense sticks - - given to a teacher

90 - 1   Ring at Ratchadamnoen Stadium
92 - 3   Bonanza Muay Thai Training Camp, Khao Yai, Nakorn Ratchasima Province to the N.E. of Bangkok

96 - 7   A fighter and his manager prostrate themselves on the floor before going up to the ring at Lumpini Stadium

106 - 7 Removal of the head circlet and marigold garland prior to starting a bout

*Photographs by courtesy of the National Archives of Thailand

What our readers are saying about....
MUAY THAI: A Living Legacy

"*Muay Thai: A Living Legacy* is a definitive introduction to one of the world's great martial arts."
CFW Enterprises, Inside Kung-fu Magazine

"What magnificent photography! Fascinating and informative text. I hope you publish more such books."
John Pilcher, C&T Publishing

"The book is an excellent presentation of old Muay Thai and the modern Ring Sport today. A 'must read' for the Muay Thai enthusiast!"
Duke Roufus, Wisconsin
Professional Fighter K-1/ Muay Thai

"This is the most comprehensive book that I have ever read on the subject of Muay Thai."
Ryan Blackorby, Illinois
TBA-USA Instructor

"After having read *Muay Thai: A Living Legacy*, I believe that it will become the industry standard for many years to come."
Stevie Nisbet
Scottish Amateur Muay Thai Association

"*Muay Thai: A Living Legacy*, is an easy reference guide to particular things that students miss when learning outside of Thailand. Congratulations on a well-done work and when the time is right I will look forward to another issue."
Marc D. Meltzer, Massachusetts

"*Muay Thai: A Living Legacy*, is a book project long overdue. Thoroughly researched and illustrated with high quality photos, this book sets the standards for all others concerning Thai Boxing and any other Thai art. This book is easily accessible as an introduction to Muay Thai for beginners, and functions as a reference work for long time practitioners."
Alex Bay, California
TBA-USA Instructor
Professor, Stanford University

"I can say it is one of the best martial arts books that I have seen. It is very complete in terms of the history, culture and techniques. The photography is excellent and the sequences of photos, which accompany the explanations of the techniques, make it easy to understand and follow."
Josephine Jackson, Florida
TBA-USA Instructor

"This book has to be the best book I have ever seen on Muay Thai."
Al Oakley, UK On-Line Fight Shop

"Your book is amazing! Being an American and searching for a 'traditional' Muay Thai school/camp has been a daunting experience. The information in your book sheds an amazing informative light and takes some of the question out of where I'm going to study."
Daniel Noss, California

"I truly enjoyed reading *Muay Thai: A Living Legacy*. In the United States, unfortunately, we have little exposure to the art of Muay Thai. This book has been extremely valuable in gaining a better understanding of the art."
Alfred Woodson, United States

"I think that you have published the ultimate introductory text about Muay Thai. The layout of each chapter is simple and easy to read. I found the content to be very informative, the text and graphics excellent."
Nelson Hamilton, California
Referee/Writer

"I think your book is the BEST!! I love the HONEST and open way that you all presented the material. I have learned so much from this book and I know it will quickly become a type of 'Bible' for Muay Thai in America and beyond."
Daniel C. Docto, California
Concord Kickboxing Club

"I give the book two thumbs up and an A+ because it explains the traditions and philosophy of Muay Thai and it also explains the Muay Thai techniques in great details...Last but not least, it comes with an awesome Wai Khru Ram Muay poster."
Rodney Ambunan, San Diego

"The book was fantastic; it does give in depth information on not only the history of Muay Thai, but in depth visual & written explanation on how to apply Muay Thai techniques. It has been an excellent read so far, one of the best martial arts books I have seen to date."
Sam Powell Jr., Oklahoma

"Honestly, I loved this book. For someone who is without a 'full-time' instructor, this book is a must!"
Mike Mattox, Illinois
Owner / Head Instructor
Championship Karate & Kickboxing

"Rating: 5 out of 5...the quality of the publication is sure to impress. *Muay Thai: A Living Legacy* is unbelievable...this is the bible for Thai boxing...a must-have for anyone interested in Muay Thai."
Mike Popp, Ultimate Athlete Magazine

MUAY THAI

A Living Legacy

Punch

The fighter in blue shorts
extends a Straight Punch
(p.146) while his opponent
tries unsuccessfully to
counter with the Lead
Knee Bomb (p.200).

MUAY THAI

A Living Legacy

Punch

As the fighter in red shorts attacks at close quarters with the Rear High Round Kick (p.212) his opponent seizes the chance to extend a Straight Punch (p.146).

A Living Legacy

MHAI THAI

Elbow Strike

The Straight Knee-Kick (p.186) of the fighter in red shorts is foiled by his opponent s well-aimed Horizontal Elbow Strike (p.164).

Knee Kick

The fighter in blue shorts attempt to counter a Straight Knee Kick (p.184) with a Low Round Kick (p.216) is mistimed and so fails.

Photograph by Jeremy Skaggs

MUAY THAI

A Living Legacy

Lumphini Stadium
March, 2004

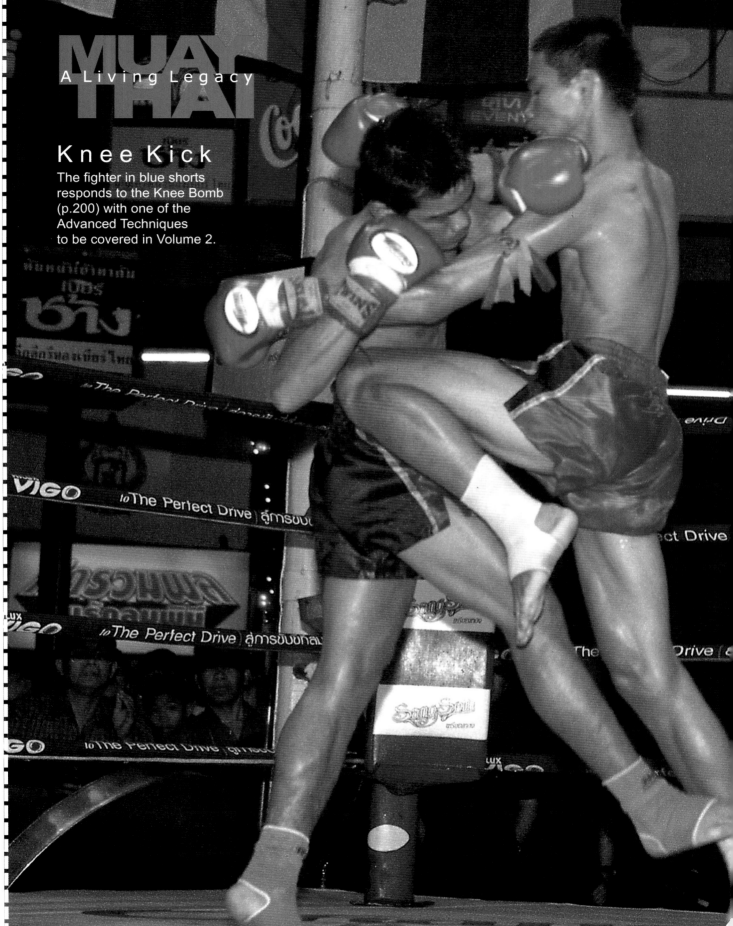

MUAY THAI

A Living Legacy

Knee Kick

The fighter in blue shorts
responds to the Knee Bomb
(p.200) with one of the
Advanced Techniques
to be covered in Volume 2.

Spry Books

MUAY THAI
A Living Legacy

Kick

The Rear High Round Kick (p.212) of the fighter in red shorts is blocked by a knee/arm combination (No.8, p.275).

MUAY THAI
A Living Legacy

Kick

The dramatic Rear High Round Kick (p.212) of the fighter on the right is effectively blocked by his opponent (No.2, p.273).

Spry Books

MUAY THAI
A Living Legacy

Foot-Thrust

While the fighter in blue shorts is in the preparatory *Yaang Sam Khum* (p.126), his opponent successfully attacks with the Straight Foot Thrust (p.237).

The Book Team

Pitsaporn "Kat" Prayukvong: Managing Editor & Researcher

Born in Bangkok, Kat has always had a love of reading and when growing up spent many hours at a city-center printers and publishers, absorbing the process of turning words into books. She studied Communications at Illinois State University, being the president of the Thai Students' Association from 1997- 8. After graduating with a B.Sc. she returned to Thailand and embarked on her first major project, *Muay Thai: A Living Legacy* doing all the hours of painstaking research, supervising the studio sessions and generally being at the helm of the whole project. She hopes to follow this up not only with two further volumes in the same series but also with other culture-oriented books.

Lesley & Wilat Junlakan: Writer/ Editor & Assistant Editor

A husband-and-wife team, Wilat Junlakan, a native of Surat-thani, in the south of Thailand, and a graduate of the province's teacher-training college, met his wife-to-be, Lesley, an M.A. in English Literature from Manchester, England, when she was lecturing at Thammasat University, Bangkok. They married in 1988 and, after spending 10 years in Japan, where Lesley taught English and Cross-Cultural Communication at the National Institute of Fitness and Sports in Kagoshima Prefecture, they returned to Thailand in April 2000.

From now on, Wilat and Lesley plan to divide their time between their house in Bangkok and a self-sufficiency small-holding in Surat-thani, writing and illustrating a variety of books and free-lancing as translators / interpreters on demand. They are both proficient in three languages: English, Thai and Japanese.

Phitsanu Kusolwong: Chief Consultant

A native of Ayutthya, Ajarn Phitsanu has a B.Sc. in Physical Education, International Sports Trainer diploma from the U.S. Sports Academy and a Sports Science qualification. At 13, he started to train in Muay Thai under *Khru* Luang and was selected by the Sports Authority of Thailand to demonstrate the arts of Muay Thai and Krabi Krabong in the 1st International Arts and Culture Fair in Germany. Since then, he has demonstrated these two martial arts in many other countries including Japan and South Africa. He has attained the 5th dan in the World Taekwondo Federation, was the first person in Thailand to be awarded a black belt in Hapkido and has also studied judo and karate. Currently, he teaches sports and martial arts at schools and gyms around Bangkok and is a committee member of the Taekwondo Association of Thailand.

Surachai "Chai" Sirisute: Consultant

The eldest of eight children, and the only boy, *Ajarn* Chai started to train in Muay Thai at the tender age of 6 or 7 and went on to fight competitively in over seventy Muay Thai contests and a score of Western boxing bouts. In 1968, he went to live permanently in the United States, where he later founded and became the president of the Thai Boxing Association of the USA (TBA-USA) which now has affiliated groups in Mexico, Europe, Australia and elsewhere. By 1982, he had a sufficiently large and skilled group of fighters to be able to bring an American team to Thailand to compete in the Muay Thai World Championships. He has instructed dignitaries and stars, statesmen and sportsmen, in the art of Muay Thai and now travels the world to teach seminars and generally promote not only Muay Thai but also Thailand itself.

Thi-tinan Pongcharoen: Graphic Designer

Born in Nonthaburi Province on the north-western edge of Bangkok, Thi-tinan has worked as a free-lance graphic designer of books, magazines and other forms of printed material for over 10 years. Much of his work has met with great acclaim, in particular *"Precious"*, a book on Buddhist amulets, and a brochure which he produced for UNESCO. A highly private person who shuns attention and publicity, Thi-tinan loves the great outdoors, especially mountains and the sea, and his hobbies include photography and watching movies.

Vichian Poosiri: Photographer

Born in Roi-Et Province in Thailand's north-east, Vichian Poosiri graduated in physics before going to America to study photography and fine arts. He was a cofounder of "La Democrat", a liberal newspaper which played a leading role in the overthrow of Thailand's military regime in 1970. While on the staff of the German Embassy in Bangkok, he become the managing-editor of a men's entertainment magazine and in 1983 founded "*Fai Glangkuen*", a night-life and entertainment periodical, of which he is still the editor/publisher. He also free-lances as a photographer for other publications and enjoys a high reputation for the quality and form of his pictures.

Yongyut Keeratiratanalak: Assistant photographer

A native of Bangkok, Yongyut is a graduate in Communicatin Design from Srinakarinwirot University. *Muay Thai: A Living Legacy* is his first major photographic project and he had particular responsibility for the location shots, especially the International *Wai Khru* Collection. Now freelancing as a graphic designer and photographer, Yongyut's dream is to open his own photo studio and

Kridakorn Sodprasert: Consultant

Born in Bangkok into an artistic family in 1957, Kridakorn has been interested in the art of *muay* since his childhood. His first teacher was his eldest brother, Wichanan, now an architect. Then, at the age of 16, he went to study *Muay Chaiya* with *Khru* Kaet at the suggestion of his elder brother, Wanlapit, who became an artist. After graduating from Assumption College, Kridakorn went to art college for four years before starting work as an apprentice of *Ajarn* Chakrabhand Posayakrit, a master puppet-maker, with whom he remained until the age of 30. During this time, at the funeral of *Khru* Kaet, Kridakorn met *Khru* Tong, who became his *Muay Chaiya* teacher for 14 years. While his twin brother is now a classical guitar teacher, Kridakorn, widely known as *Khru* Lek, is devoted to the fostering of Thai culture and not only makes traditional Thai puppets but also teaches *Muay Chaiya,* Thai art, dance and puppetry at his home.

Chaichalerm Naksawart: Consultant

A skilled all-rounder in a variety of martial arts, *Ajarn* Chaichalerm has a 4th dan in taekwondo and a 1st dan in hapkido. He was awarded the Princess' Cup in 1984 after winning the National *Krabi Krabong* Championship. He was the national taekwondo champion for two consecutive years (1987 and '88) and the top taekwondo coach of 1993. As far as Muay Thai is concerned, he specializes in *Muay Boran*. He currently teaches at the Martial Arts Taekwondo Academy and the Pro Martial Arts Center, both in Bangkok.

Sawang Sawangkawat: Consultant

A native of Sakon Nakorn in Thailand's north-east, Sawang is one of the most professional of all Muay Thai writers. Starting off as a reporter for a range of Muay Thai publications, by 1965 he had risen to become the director of "Boxing" magazine. He went on to be the founder and executive editor of such periodicals as *"Yod Nak Soo"* and "Fighter". Now aged 70, he is a member of the Ranking Committee of Ratchadamnoen Stadium and vice-president of the Ranking Committees of both Lumphini Stadium and The World Muay Thai Council, having been a member of the latter for more than 40 years.

Apiwat Seinaloy: Consultant

A native of Galasin Province in the north-east of Thailand, Apiwat Seinaloy took the pen-name by which he is widely known, "Wat Poothai", from the Tin-poothai district in which he was born. He came to Bangkok around the age of twenty and in the forty or more years since then he has worked as a writer or in a editorial capacity for a wide range of publications. He was the chairman of the Sports Reporters Association of Thailand for six years and is widely known in Muay Thai circles. Currently, Apiwat writes a daily Muay Thai

The Muay Thai Models

Komgrit Tongdee
Fighting under the name Komgrit Sitphraprom, Komgrit was born in 1973 and started his Muay Thai fighting career at the age of 13, taking part in 80 bouts altogether. He is now in the fourth year of an interior design course at college and dreams of combining his twin interests by becoming both a designer and a Muay Thai teacher.

Karl Jamornmarn
Born in Halifax, England, in 1961, but returning to live in Thailand two years later, Karl is an electrical engineer. Muay Thai is a hobby which he started a year ago to keep him physically fit, and he also does weight training and jogging.

Tienchai Gorging
Born in the central province of Lopburi in 1975, Tienchai came relatively late to Muay, starting training when he was 15. Of his 40 pro-Muay Thai fights, he lost 4, drew 1 and won the rest, and he won all but 7 of his 47 Western boxing bouts. He was the 1995-6 WBU Fly-Weight World Champion. He is now an instructor and wants to have his own training camp.

Tongmee Deebuapa
Born in Srisakaet Province in the north-east of Thailand in 1983, Tongmee started Muay Thai at the age of 5 or 6. He has already had 20 fights in the professional Muay Thai ring, of which he won 15, and has won all but 1 of his 11 Western boxing bouts. He trains with Tienchai Gorging and his dream is to be a WBC champion.

Additional models
Supachai Tonglimsud, Arak Amornsupasiri, Kongkiet Pasukkul, Ratee Kruakae, Nantana Pramoonsin